VANCOUVER BLUE

C3

VANCOUVER BLUE

A Life Against Crime

Wayne Cope

HARBOUR PUBLISHING

Harbour Publishing Co. Ltd.
P.O. Box 219, Madeira Park, BC, V0N 2H0
www.harbourpublishing.com

All photographs from the author's collection
Edited by Betty Keller
Cover design by Shed Simas
Text design by Mary White
Printed and bound in Canada

Harbour Publishing acknowledges the support of the Canada Council for the Arts, which last year invested $157 million to bring the arts to Canadians throughout the country. We also gratefully acknowledge financial support from the Government of Canada through the Canada Book Fund and from the Province of British Columbia through the BC Arts Council and the Book Publishing Tax Credit.

Cataloguing data available from Library and Archives Canada
ISBN 978-1-55017-699-5 (paper)
ISBN 978-1-55017-700-8 (ebook)

Note: Most names used in this book, as well as some identifying details, have been changed to protect the privacy of individuals. Other names have been changed to avoid adding to the notoriety of convicted criminals.

To Dawna, who thinks that some of my stories are as entertaining as I do, and who encouraged me to commit them to paper.

To Marge—I concede. It may have been your idea.

To Shelley Fralic for helping me turn a collection of anecdotes into a book.

To the Vancouver Police Department—it's been an honour and a privilege working with 89 percent of you (see Chapter 7, The Idiot Factor).

To Mrs. Brandon and my grade two class at Grandview Elementary School.

To my friend Victor the Knife from kindergarten— if that was you we pulverized with tear gas outside the Yaletown Postal Depot or blasted with the beanbag gun on Granville Street, I'm sorry. I didn't recognize you. It's been more than forty years.

Contents

Introduction

The Empress Hotel beer parlour, or "the Emp," is a Downtown Eastside watering hole located across the lane from the Main Street police station. Before the Vancouver Police Union built the Police Athletic Club two blocks farther north on Alexander Street, the Emp was the place for police officers to go when their shifts were over, as it offered discreet card tables for a friendly game and "last call" only meant that the staff was about to bar the door to new customers rather than require patrons to leave.

In April 1979 I had been on the job for four years and, after my shift, was at the Emp with six or seven fellow Traffic Division motorcycle trainees, drinking beer and solving all the problems of the world. Elvis had died two years earlier, and after heated debate I had achieved consensus with the group that Johnny Cash was now the world's greatest living musical entertainer. Having resolved that issue, one of the crew asked me if I had any thoughts about what I wanted to do with my career over the course of the next thirty years. I answered, "Absolutely. I would like to ride the motorcycles for a while, walk the beat, work undercover, continue shooting with the pistol team, be part of a surveillance unit, work as a dog master and investigate murders. I've got no aspirations of becoming commissioned as an officer, and if I retire as a sergeant in charge of a good squad of people, that would be just fine with me." He seemed surprised and said, "You sure seem to have it all worked out." I responded, "I don't know about having it all worked out, but I don't want to look back thirty years from now and say, "That was sure boring."

It was rarely boring.

I enjoy experiencing new things and doing what others haven't done. I got my scuba licence when I was fifteen years old and have dived the Pacific West Coast, the Great Barrier Reef, the Cozumel Wall, the Chaak Tun Cenote in the Yucatan, the Gulf of California, Bali and the Canary Islands. At the time of this writing I have been on a pilgrimage to Jim Morrison's grave at the Père Lachaise Cemetery in Paris five times, run with the bulls in Pamplona on twelve occasions

Ever since my time in Mrs. Brandon's grade two class at Grandview Elementary School, I wanted to be a policeman and scuba diver.

and, at fifty-five below zero, witnessed Lance Mackey and his dog-sled team win the Iditarod in Nome for the third consecutive time. Each adventure has not much to do with the other, but perhaps they offer insight into the type of person who has written this book.

The three founding principles of policing have remained the same since 1829, when Sir Robert Peel developed the metropolitan model in London, England. First, the police are accountable to the public. Second, the effectiveness of a police department is not measured by the number of arrests made, but by an absence of crime. Third, the most important part of establishing a credible police service is establishing and maintaining the public trust.

In the Beginning

Meet the Family

My father, Alfred Cope, was from Winnipeg and left home at fifteen to work in the northern mines of Churchill. He had only completed grade six, but when joking about his education, he would say that he had done half of grade twelve. When meeting people who were from Manitoba, he would bait them with: "There is only one good road in Winnipeg. That's the road heading out of town." His father, Albert Cope, was a wounded veteran of the First World War, and his uncle Llewellyn had been killed near Elverdinghe Chateau in Flanders on August 24, 1917.

After working in the mines, Dad rode the rails to the West Coast, where he took a job as a sawyer at the Hammond Mill in Pitt Meadows. His nickname was "Cash" because he always carried a large wad of bills to negotiate any spontaneous deal that came his way. Never one for maintaining his property, whenever something broke or needed replacing, he would comment, "Oh, well, it's only money, and I got lots."

My mother, Margaret Sweet, was born in Vernon, BC. Her father was a mill worker and her mother stayed at home to care for her brothers and sisters. Margaret had moved to New Westminster to enter nursing school at Essondale Hospital when she met Dad at a dance at the Harris Road Community Hall in 1952. They were married a short time later. They had four children, two boys and two girls. The girls became nurses; the boys became policemen.

An update on the police side of the author's family so far includes, wife: senior director, Vancouver Police Department; brother: inspector, VPD; father-in-law: chief constable-retired, VPD; brother-in-law: sergeant, VPD; nephew: constable, VPD; another nephew: Vancouver civilian peace officer in the VPD Information Management Section; niece's husband: constable, VPD; cousin and black sheep of the family: staff sergeant, Canadian Pacific Railway Police. Recently, at a very large family gathering, I commented to another brother-in-law, who owns a construction company, "Did you know that you are the only person in this room who doesn't work for the government?" He responded, "I just took a contract from the Burnaby School Board."

I Blame Television

I was born in Saint Mary's Hospital in New Westminster and raised in Vancouver's "Little Italy" on Commercial Drive, which in those days was a thriving working-class neighbourhood populated by new European immigrants. However, we lived across the street from Clark Park, which was the local gathering place for thieves and hoods known as "Clark Parkers," many of whom graduated to become outlaw motorcycle-gang members. In later years I learned that the Vancouver Police Department solved the Clark Park problem by creating the "H" or Heavy Squad. Dressed in dark plainclothes with signature fedora hats, the members of the squad would sweep through the park several times in the course of an evening, using baseball bats to encourage the thugs to leave the area. When the problem was miraculously solved, an elderly female resident living across from the park commented to reporters, "It seems as though an older gang has taken over the park, and they are so much more polite than the other group."

My friends were Joe Barsilli, Billy Turkanoff and Victor the Knife. I don't remember what Victor's last name was, but he earned his unfortunate sobriquet on our first day of kindergarten when a discussion with the teacher about whether or not he would participate in nap time deteriorated into an ugly incident. He wasn't there for the second day of kindergarten. Joe and Billy were relatively tame. I remember sitting in the lunchroom at Grandview Elementary School enjoying my daily Wonder Bread sandwich with peanut butter and jam that I had just taken out of my Roy Rogers lunch kit. Watching the other kids chewing on home-made filone, pane Siciliano or ciabatta heaped with provolone and prosciutto, I thought, Boy, eating that rotten-smelling stuff . . . they must be poor.

Television was black and white with no cable or remote control, but we watched *Bonanza* every Sunday, and *Gunsmoke*, *Have Gun—Will Travel* (and no, Alex Trebek, the first name of Paladin was not "Wire," even though his card said, "Wire Paladin, San Francisco"—the reference meant "*Telegraph* Paladin in San Francisco"), *Dragnet* and *Sea Hunt* during the week.

One of our favourite pastimes was running through the neighbourhood playing "cops and robbers." Mom alleges that when I was on my way out to play, she would always caution me to "play the cop, not the robber." I don't recall this, but I have no evidence to the contrary. One day in 1962, when I was in grade two, our teacher, Mrs. Brandon, had the children come up to the front of the class one by one and tell everybody what they wanted to do when they grew up. I was seven years old when I stood before the class and proudly proclaimed that I wanted to scuba dive and be a policeman. My mother claims credit for my career; I blame James Arness and Richard Boone.

President Lupo

In 1973, after graduating from Gladstone Secondary School, I enrolled in the Criminal Justice Program at Langara College in Vancouver. The instructor was Ian Bruce Campbell, and I really enjoyed the classes he taught. He had been a bobby in Great Britain and then served with the British military to put down the Mau Mau uprising in Kenya before immigrating to Canada, where he joined a small municipal police department back east. My classmates and I enjoyed diverting him from the mundane curriculum so that he would recount the more interesting experiences of his past. He once told us of the time he and his squad

While studying Criminology at VCC Langara, my class created this jacket crest.

15

were out in the jungle on an anti-rebel patrol when they were ambushed. One of his friends on the patrol, badly burned in the firefight, asked his troop mates to kill him, as he could not deal with the pain and disfigurement. They carried the soldier to base hospital, where he was treated and survived. Several times since then that injured soldier thanked Campbell for not complying with his request. Campbell said that this was one of the most difficult decisions he ever made.

After he came to Canada, the town where Campbell served as a police constable was suffering thefts from parking meters. It was a particularly embarrassing crime because the location of the thefts was so public. Campbell staked out a likely row of parking meters near the town square in the early hours of the morning, then hid to await the thieves' arrival. When he saw two shadowy figures emptying the coin meters, he moved in and discovered that the petty crooks were, in fact, fellow police officers from his own department. He told our class that he was surprised at the way some of his co-workers treated him as a result of arresting these two thieves. He still advocated doing the right thing, but he advised us that "whistle blowers" should have a thick skin. The arrest of his two co-workers likely precipitated his move to the West Coast. Ian Campbell made a great contribution to public safety, training hundreds of students who would go on to serve with distinction as peace officers throughout the province.

Other than Campbell's classes, I found academia boring and spent a lot of my time at Langara supplementing my lifeguard's income (I had been a lifeguard at various pools and beaches in the city since I was fifteen) by playing blackjack in the cafeteria. I was also attracted to student politics, and in the spring semester of 1974 I was elected vice-president of the student union. When the president stepped down later in the year, I took over as head of the council. Some years later, when I was serving in the Vancouver Police Department's Traffic Division, a group of us were having breakfast in a restaurant on Denman Street when I was approached by Betsy Dennison, a fellow former student representative. We had a few words, and when she left the table, the guys asked, "Where do you know her from?" I told them that we had been on student council together, and when I became president, she had taken over the office of vice-president. And that was it. From that moment on I was "the Pres." It was written on my locker and DynaTaped to the back of my motorcycle helmet.

In policing, many people have nicknames, and you hope and pray that if you acquire one, it won't be too humiliating. I got away pretty lucky. Some of the good and bad ones included: Spanky, Frank, McStabb, McSnapper, the Poisoned Dwarf, Renatta the She-Wolf of the SS, the Outlaw, the Commander, Skipper, Tripod, the Peeper, Dog-balls, Big Yellow Bird, RAM, Cathy Alphabet, the Schnozz, the Horseman, the Purple Onion, the Poodle and Electra. One of the constables acquired an unfortunate nickname that followed him throughout his career. On one dark and stormy night, four of us were wearing our yellow rain slickers as we worked a roadblock in the West End, when Constable Jim Davidson arrested a driver for being impaired. As the other three of us huddled together watching the formalities, Jim dealt with the driver, who refused to take a breathalyzer test. One requirement of Canadian law is that to make a legal arrest, a constable must formally identify himself, touch the offender and tell him or her the true reason for the arrest. Davidson touched the drunk and said, "You understand that I am a police officer?" The drunk responded, "A police officer . . . a police officer? You don't look like no police officer. You look like a duck." And that's how the legend of "the Duck" was born.

My own nickname didn't change until years later, when I was a patrol sergeant and my crew decided that I reminded them of "Lupo"—not the lone, silent predator, skirting the shadows, waiting to lash out at criminal prey, but a psychopathic, meat-cleaver-swinging butcher that a local illustrator was trying to make into a notorious cartoon figure. I still have the T-shirt. The name stuck even after I left the Patrol Division, but fortunately, very few remembered that the full nickname was "Lupo the Butcher."

Late in 1973, while I was attending Langara College, I passed the exam for the Vancouver Police Department's Reserve Unit. When I had my interview, the inspector checked my score and advised me that there would be no reason to re-write the exam should I wish to apply for the Regular Force when I turned twenty-one, which was then the minimum age requirement.

Oakalla Prison

In the spring of 1974 I was 18 years of age, and I applied for summer work at Oakalla Prison Farm in Burnaby, BC. I asked the prison personnel officer if I could do the widest possible range of jobs rather than be assigned to one unit. As I had already been trained in the use of the Smith & Wesson Model 10 .38 calibre revolver by the Vancouver Police Department, my first assignment was to work the prison's west wing wall. For this assignment I carried a Winchester lever-action .30-30 that I hadn't been trained on but had seen John Wayne use several times in the movies.

Later I worked the mobile patrol, the isolation unit (located under the piggery) and the west wing lock-up.

One of the first pieces of advice I was given while working at Oakalla came from a grizzled old jailer. He advised, "Don't be nice to the scrotes. When there is a riot, the friendly guards are the first ones they take hostage." (Short for scrotum, "scrote" is a Vancouver Eastside term used to describe worthless scum.) Less than a year later, social worker Mary Steinhauser and fourteen other staffers were taken hostage by prisoners at the BC Penitentiary in New Westminster. Forty hours into the hostage taking, prison guards stormed the barricade and opened fire. Steinhauser was killed by gunfire, and one of the hostage takers was seriously wounded.

Pocket identification I was issued while working in the summer of 1974 at Oakalla Prison Farm.

The west wing was the most dangerous place in Oakalla to work. Prisoners were held there awaiting trial, so they had no way of knowing what, if any, sentence they would be facing, and tempers flared with little warning. It was here that I met Eddy Haymour, generally considered to be one of Canada's few truly political prisoners. In 1971, he had purchased Rattlesnake Island on Okanagan Lake near Peachand, BC, and proceeded with his plan of turning the island into an Arabian Nights–themed amusement park, to the chagrin of local and provincial politicians. But his project was torpedoed and he was later arrested for making threats, then ultimately incarcerated in Oakalla.

Haymour was by trade a barber and he held court daily, offering advice and wisdom at the prison barbershop. One day, along with seven or eight prisoners, I was being entertained by Haymour's theories about the nature of the world when he told me, "The reason all of these men are criminals is because they are all bastards. None of them know their fathers." He pointed to each of the prisoners in turn, and rather than be offended, each offered a brief comment that supported Haymour's statement. In fact, none of them knew their fathers.

Haymour later sold Rattlesnake Island back to the provincial government for forty thousand dollars and was found not guilty of the charges against him. He was ultimately freed and in the fall of 1975 went home to Lebanon. A few months later he and his cousins seized the Canadian Embassy in Beirut. He negotiated his way back to Canada, where he had been assured that the federal government would assist him in processing his claim for compensation. In 1986 the BC Supreme Court ruled that the BC government had conspired against him and his theme park and awarded him $250,000 in compensation. He didn't get his island back, but he built Castle Haymour, now Peachland Castle, on Highway 97 in Peachland, BC.

Working at Oakalla taught me three things: One, don't be nice to the scrotes. Two, criminality generally occurs as a result of a breakdown of the family unit. Three, don't ever work in a jail.

In 1974 the age requirement for Vancouver City Police recruits was reduced from twenty-one to nineteen, the height restriction was eliminated and the minimum education standard was raised to secondary school graduation instead of grade eleven. By this time the days of twirling a Fraternal Order of Masons ring while sitting for a job interview were long gone, and Vancouver was breaking new ground by diversifying its hiring practices. However, what really increased the multicultural nature of the force was not just the new progressive attitude about hiring people who reflected the makeup of the community; it was the elimination of the height requirement. Demanding that recruit candidates be at least six feet tall had acted as a silent barrier to employment for many Asian groups. Now recruits were only required to be physically fit and in excellent health. From that time on, whenever the department marched in parades, you no longer saw a sea of white faces.

Don Winterton, the new chief constable, was heavily promoting a program of neighbourhood policing, which meant assigning a contingent of officers to individual neighbourhood-support offices. This program, coupled with union demands that a higher percentage of police cars be manned by two officers, resulted in a hiring boom. Normally the VPD would hire about thirty members a year to cover attrition, but in 1975 more than 160 officers were hired, bringing the total number on payroll to about 850.

That September I came to Inspector Don MacGregor's office to advise him that my birthday was on October 19, and then I would be good to go. At that time armed reserve officers accompanied regular police members who would have otherwise been in one-man police cars. At the end of shift the regular officer would submit a fitness report that would go on the reserve officer's record of service. MacGregor said that he would consider my application in about a year, when there were more of these fitness reports on my service record for him to scrutinize. From that day on, I was out in the patrol cars three times a week. In December, with a stack of recommendations spilling from my file folder, I re-attended MacGregor's office, hoping he had forgotten that he told me to come back in a year.

On February 20, 1975, I received a letter stating:

Dear Sir:

This is to inform you that you have been chosen a member of this force and you are instructed to report to the Police Training Academy, HMCS *Discovery*, Stanley Park, Vancouver, at 7:30 a.m. on March 10, 1975. Please bring your birth certificate with you.

The Police Academy, 1975

My partner: "I have two degrees from the University of Saskatchewan. This police department isn't capable of writing a test I can't pass." (He didn't pass the test.)

My first day at the Police Academy was March 10, 1975. Up until that time, Vancouver had run its own academy, attended by municipal officers from all over the province, but I was a member of class one of the new Provincial Police College. Recruits from six of the twelve municipal police departments were represented at the largest collection of officers ever trained at one time in British Columbia. In fact, class one was so large that it had been split into four units to be more manageable.

On the morning of the first day, the inspector in charge made a speech to the group acknowledging that though 107 recruits was a very large number to train, he was confident that, because of the extensive background checks that had been done and the quality of recruit selected, all 107 would graduate. Except there weren't 107 recruits gathered there that morning waiting to be sworn in. There were 106. The previous evening one of Vancouver's pre-recruits had been the subject of a police check when he was found exposing himself to prostitutes in Vancouver's Downtown Eastside. They advised him not to show up for work the next day.

Training at the Provincial Police College was to more closely resemble a university environment than the traditional police academy, and completion of some of the courses earned recruits transferable university credits. As well as the usual training in law, police procedure, pursuit driving, traffic studies, firearms and physical education, we had courses in psychology and multiculturalism. Our training consisted of three "blocks" of study, and the first of them, which was fourteen weeks long, included our VPD orientation and ended with a mile-and-a-half run on the last day.

Corporal Steve Sidney was our drill instructor, and on the first day he walked back and forth, inspecting our class. As he passed me, he said, "Cope, haircut." So I thought, okay, this is Monday. On the weekend I'll hit the barbershop and everybody will be happy. At Tuesday morning parade Sidney stopped in front of me and said, "Cope, didn't I tell you to get your hair cut for today?" Well no, not really, I thought. There was no timeline given for what had appeared to be more of a request or suggestion than an order. Before I had a chance to vocalize my defence, Sidney said, "Okay, Cope, have your hair cut by tomorrow or don't bother showing up." This really wasn't the good first impression I wanted to make on my second day at the Academy, but I don't think an explanation would have mattered anyway.

Attrition was brutal in those first weeks of training. Two or three times a week, a recruit would be asked to report to the office and bring his or her books. I sat in the front row of our class, fourth desk from the right. When the first two recruits sitting at the far left of the front row were sacked, the next person in line picked up all of his books and quietly relocated to the back.

One day when I was sitting with one of the policewomen in our class, she said she wanted my advice about something personal. I said, "Sure, go ahead." She told me that when the examination marks were posted on the wall and she went up to check her scores, one of our classmates, a former armoured-car guard, would come up behind her and grind his pelvis into her hip. As she was telling me the story, another policewoman overheard and joined us to ask, "Is he doing that to you, too?" The question was whether or not I thought this was normal behaviour, and whether they should report it. First, I joked, "Define normal," but then I reconsidered and told them to report it. They didn't report him, but a different sort of offence about a year later finished his police career.

It happened when members of our recruit class participated in a "Take a social worker to work" day. I guess the idea was to see the community from another professional perspective. "Constable Pelvis" and his worker met with two other constables for lunch in company with their respective social workers. In the course of the conversation, one of the social workers commented that it must be frustrating to deal with criminals who commit horrible crimes and can't be prosecuted because there just isn't enough evidence to charge them. Pelvis confided that, if this were the case, he would just plant some evidence on the criminal to get him off the street. When the social workers reported the conversation, a quick investigation was done, and Pelvis was asked to bring his books to the office. The two other constables at the lunch were also interviewed, and it was pointed out to them that they should have spoken up. I know both officers, who are highly respected and now retired from policing, and they told me, "Wayne, we just didn't hear him say it."

Jim Roddick was another odd duck. He had previously served as a police officer with Vancouver, quit over some controversy and then returned. I later learned that the controversy concerned the arrest of an armed suspect who had just been involved in a robbery. Roddick had cornered the suspect in a lane from which there was no exit. Time passed, cover units arrived, and ultimately a dialogue was established with the suspect, who refused to surrender. The exchange went on and on and on and finally the negotiator asked, "So why won't you give up? We guarantee your safety and you will be taken into custody." The crook yelled back, "Yeah? Well, that's what the first guy said, but every time I stood up, he fired another shot at me."

Roddick was one of those "been everywhere, done everything" guys. Though guardedly friendly, he spewed negativity about just about every aspect of the new police college. One morning he told me that he would be happy to talk to me about all of the problems he was observing with this completely dysfunctional academic program, but that any conversation we had would have to take place outside because the classrooms were all electronically bugged. After we went outside and he told me what was wrong with the college, I told him that the real problem with the college was that the director and his staff running the program weren't getting proper feedback from credible people who really knew what was going on. I told him that the director would probably welcome the type of ideas and concerns he had just expressed to me. Roddick asked, "Do you really think I should talk to him?" I said, "I think you should go to his office and tell him exactly what you have told me here this morning."

Roddick said, "You really think so?" I said, "I think you owe it to yourself and everybody here." Roddick got up, walked over to the open door and turned left to walk down the hallway toward the director's office. That was thirty-nine years ago, and I haven't seen him since.

As a recruit, I recognized that in some areas people with previous police experience had a leg up on the others during training. When I had taken firearms training in the reserves, I had been taught Olympic-style one-handed shooting with .38-calibre Smith & Wesson Model 10 revolvers firing moderate-velocity, lead, round-nose bullets. But the reserves had a three-strike rule. After receiving training, if you failed to shoot a qualifying score in three attempts, you failed the reserve-police program. I had failed twice, then qualified by the skin of my teeth on my third attempt. As I hadn't wanted to ever worry again about being a poor marksman, I had begun to practice the new two-handed style of shooting both with the reserves and at Oakalla's outdoor range. As a result, I usually had the highest firearms scores in my recruit class, and in 1976 I won first place in the Service Weapon Event at the BC Provincial Combat Shooting Championship. In 1981 and 1982 I won first place in the Expert Division of the Provincial Combat Shooting Championship and won trophies in the team events.

Anything I had learned in the reserves, I kept to myself. There's little that's more annoying than some know-it-all recruit who wants to tell everybody about how it really is out on the road. Chuck Hadley was and is a good friend of mine who also had police-reserve experience but didn't follow the same code of silence. He would ask incessant questions about every aspect of the lecture topics. At one point a frustrated instructor confronted one of his questions with "Hadley,

I know that you already know the answer to that question."
Hadley responded, "Yes, I do, but I am asking on behalf of
others in the class who may not."

On the first day of physical training, Hadley wore brand
new blue running shoes with his running gear as opposed to
the white ones we had been directed to purchase. The physical training instructor advised him to henceforth present
himself in white runners like all of the rest of his classmates
when taking physical education. Hadley's response was "I just
spent forty-five dollars on these runners, and if you think that
I am going to buy another pair because these are the wrong
colour, you are out of your mind."

The corporal responded, "Hadley, you will report for duty
tomorrow with footwear of the correct colour or don't bother
showing up."

The next day Hadley was wearing white runners when
the class reported for parade. The corporal nodded approval,
noting Hadley's correct kit, then took his position at the
front of the class. "I have considered the issue of footwear,"
the corporal said, "and have decided from this point forward
there will be no colour restriction. Wear whatever colour you
like."

Physical training was a rigorous program that included
push-ups, sit-ups, pull-ups, self-defence, arrest techniques
and running. The scores for each activity were weighted
then added together on the day of the final test, which was
the mile-and-a-half run. I, like most of the other young men
in the class, found the training eminently survivable and,
because of the high scores we had accumulated in advance
of the run, would have passed the final test without taking it.

I found that a lot of my criminal-justice training at
Langara assisted me at the police college. I had already

memorized all of the sections of the Canadian Criminal Code that I knew would be significant and can still recite the peace officer's "powers of arrest" (then Section 450, now Section 495 of the Criminal Code of Canada) verbatim. However, attending the courses and enduring the subsequent testing was very stressful. Even though I usually scored in the top third of the class, I was very apprehensive when I approached the posted scores.

After we had finished our first block of training, we were sent out for four months with a field trainer who would assess how we applied that training on the street. The second block was eight weeks long and continued where block one left off, though it focused more on training simulations and police techniques. At the end of block two it was back out to the field, usually assigned to a senior partner for about a year.

The last block of training was a five-week-long lovefest where recruits attempted to out-bullshit each other with tales of derring-do in the rough-and-tumble world of Vancouver's street scene. (In subsequent years, block-three training was deleted from the training program.) Because of this long, ongoing training program, our graduation didn't take place until February 3, 1978. My friend Dan Dureau gave the valedictory address.

Police Patrol, 1975–79

Cedar Cottage

Since I had enrolled in the Criminal Justice Program at Langara only to prepare myself for joining the Vancouver Police Department, I left the program prior to my final term when the job with the police was offered. I was happy to move on, knowing that, if I wanted, I could eventually return to school and pick up the courses I hadn't completed. I also knew that seniority was an important issue in a union environment. As a result, I was senior to friends in my college class who stayed at Langara to complete the program, and I remained senior to all of them for the more than thirty-one years I served with the VPD.

For policing purposes, the city of Vancouver is split into four districts. District One is the northwest or downtown sector. District Two is the Downtown Eastside all the way to Boundary Road. District Three is East Vancouver, with Broadway its north boundary, Main Street the west boundary and the Fraser River the south boundary. District Four encompasses the southwest sector of the city. To identify patrol assignments, numbers one through four are used as the prefix of each car's call sign, so Car 3A21 is a car working in District Three. The Alpha in the call sign means that the unit is dayshift as opposed to Charlie (afternoons) or Echo (night shift).

For my first four years of policing I was assigned to Team 34 (Cedar Cottage) in District Three. I had pretty much spent all of my school years in the East End, so I was policing in my comfort zone. I had the same partner for four years, both of us just out of the police academy, and I'm guessing the only reason the sergeant allowed two rookies to work together was because we already had a history of making good arrests. My badge number was 652, and being my classmate, my partner, Shawn Crowther, had badge number 653, but for constables sworn in on the same day, seniority is alphabetical, so Crowther, by virtue of the alphabet, was junior to me. As senior man, I had first pick of vacation leave, while he was given every wagon-driver assignment, every jail-guard position and every dirty job that came along for a rookie to fill.

Crowther didn't like to drive, which suited me just fine. If we were assigned one of the new Plymouth Gran Fury Police Special 360 V-8 rocket ships, it was our practice to lift and reverse the air filter pan to maximize oxygen flow to the carburetor and maintain the fuel

One of my first "inside jobs" was working six months at the Cedar Cottage Community Police Office in 1976.

31

level at half a tank to minimize the vehicle weight. (This is one good reason why two twenty-year-old police officers should never be allowed to work together!) While I enjoyed driving, I never felt the need to own a new car. Police cars were always going to be faster, shinier and more expensive than anything I could ever afford. While I was in college, I had driven an old Volkswagen Bug. Then one winter evening in 1974 it was flattened to the front windshield by a new driver who thought it would be a good idea to slide northbound through a stop sign at Vancouver's Commercial/Victoria Diversion and hit me head-on while I was heading south. I replaced the Bug with a Chevrolet Vega, but its aluminum motor promptly blew up while I was crossing the Port Mann Bridge. These were the types of cars I had always owned.

I have always maintained that Sunday is a good day to do police work. First, there are fewer citizens mobile in the city because they tend to stay home with their families. Second, the police, responding to a lack of traffic and activity (and hockey on the tube), tend to stand down from aggressive and proactive policing. Third, drug addicts (who commit most of Vancouver's crime), driven by a need for narcotics that doesn't recognize a calendar, are as active as ever. Thus, one has a quarry-rich environment with few hunters.

One Sunday, Crowther was away and I was assigned to a late dayshift working a one-man car. I presented myself to the duty corporal to pick up my radio and car keys and was told that there were no vehicles available. I gave him a what's-next? shrug, and he thought for a second. Then, relenting, he said, "Okay, the sergeant's brand new car has just come in from the paint and decal shop. He's not in today so you can take it out. Don't put a scratch on it."

About 11 a.m. I was southbound on Renfrew Street, approaching 22nd Avenue; to my left was Renfrew Pool, where in my previous life I had spent a lot of time lifeguarding. That's when I saw a 1956 Chevrolet Bel Air coming toward me. The sunlight gleamed off its custom lacquer, and its chrome sparkled and flashed. What a perfect day to cruise the city in your polished ride, I thought. That hot rod was shinier than the spanking new Plymouth Fury that I was driving. But as the Chevy passed me going northbound, I looked through the driver's-side window to see two drug addicts in the front seat, both higher than a kite. I hit the lights, turned on the siren and broadcast the pursuit. They went faster and I went faster, and the chase was on. We finally ended up back near 20th and Renfrew, where they turned west. I took the corner, tires screaming, and saw gravel, dust and smoke coming out of an alley. At the lane intersection an older fellow was mowing his lawn, and like a traffic bobby he waved his arms and pointed down the lane. I took that corner at about sixty kilometres an hour and was accelerating when I hit the telephone pole. This was in the days before seat belts, and the sudden stop launched me into the rear-view mirror, where I left a four-inch strip of my scalp.

Sitting in the rubble, I looked up through the smashed windshield to see that the lane terminated another thirty metres farther up, where it came to a T and turned east. The classic Chevy had failed to make the turn and had embedded itself in somebody's garage. Both car doors were open. I got out of my car and ran to the vehicle and then eastbound toward Renfrew Park. When the dog squad arrived in company with other units, I was taken to the nearby fire hall for preliminary bandaging before a patrol unit transported me to Vancouver General Hospital. Before they took me away I told the policeman, "Drive past the sergeant's car. I want to have a look at it." When we arrived back in the alley, a tow truck driver had already winched the wreck up onto a flatbed and was shovelling extraneous pieces from the road into the front seat through the smashed-out windshield. The telephone pole was snapped but still standing. Meanwhile, the dog master had tracked the driver of the Bel Air into the gully in Renfrew Park, where he was arrested. Periodically I would drive past the accident scene. The telephone pole, though clearly broken, was not replaced for many years. And I would smile as I recalled the corporal handing me the keys to the sergeant's car and warning me not to put a scratch on it.

About 9 a.m. on another lovely Sunday, Crowther and I were northbound on Commercial Drive approaching 12th Avenue when we noticed a loony-looking white male walking northbound on the west side of the street. He was wearing a loose-fitting shirt and cut-off jeans. Noticing (and I maintain that Crowther noticed it first) that the loon had an erection that bulged up the front of his cut-offs, I did a U-turn and pulled over to the curb to talk to him. We did a quick record check over the radio and were told that there was an arrest warrant in effect for him for rape. Who would have thought?

One Monday Crowther and I were driving north-bound on Knight Street at about 28th Avenue when a call came across the radio about two men fighting in a parking lot at 25th. We rolled into the lot a minute later and found a fellow in his seventies standing over a drug addict in his mid-twenties who was lying on his back, shaking. There was a big hole, a really big hole, dead centre in his chest and an old .455-calibre Enfield-style revolver lying on the ground between the old man and the addict. The pool of blood on the ground was big and getting bigger. The older fellow said,

"I was taking the money from the church to the bank over there." I did chest compressions and Crowther did mouth-to-mouth resuscitation. That was the first time I gave first aid to an injured party who didn't make it.

Later I went down to speak to the investigators in Homicide to check on the status of the case. I spoke to one of the most senior members of the team, who was smoking a cigar at his desk. He looked up, noticed that I was visibly shaken and said, "Kid, that guy was shot right through the aorta. If it had happened in the operating room of St. Paul's Hospital, it wouldn't have mattered. He was a goner. You did everything you could." This was reassuring. I went on to ask about the gun. To me it had seemed to be the type of gun that an old "navy guy" would have in his closet and bring out only when escorting money from the church to the bank. The old detective thought about it for a second and then said, "Nah. It's much more likely that we're going to find out that old hand cannon was stolen in some break-in." He was probably right, and I never heard anything further about the file.

What's the Score?

Early in my police career I started counting the instances I administered first aid to the seriously injured. Total number of times: fourteen. Total number of survivors: none. When I got to number thirteen, I thought that this would be the turning point, that thirteen would actually become some-body's lucky number. Wrong. Then I thought number fourteen would break the curse. Wrong. At number fourteen I was about halfway through my career, but by then I began to recognize when it was just too late to help.

The first time someone died despite my attempts was the robbery suspect with the big hole in his chest. Another serious-injury call that I'll never forget was a case of sudden infant death syndrome. Though I've given it a lot of thought, other than the fact that I kept a running tally, I have no memory of the specifics relating to any of the others. But as I didn't count those who probably would have survived without immediate medical intervention, I figure it was my willingness to do first aid in cases where there were grievous injuries that probably contributed to my lack of success. But I never hesitated to take action in crisis situations and enjoyed the role of problem solver.

Before the Hostage Negotiation Unit was formally attached to the Emergency Response Team, negotiations were simply handled by people who had taken the training. In 1982 I took the Crisis Management Instructors Course at the Federal Training Academy in Ottawa, and as a result, I was called in to talk two "jumpers" off of the Lions Gate Bridge, and I persuaded one barricaded gunman to surrender to the police. One of the strategies I used to talk people off of bridges was to tell them that of over 1,500 people who had jumped from the Golden Gate Bridge in San Francisco, thirty-two had survived (as of 2013 the total is thirty-four). I would go on to tell the would-be jumper that when each of the thirty-two was interviewed about their suicide attempt, every single one of them said that, as they fell to what they believed would be their certain death, they had changed their minds. On the two occasions that I used this strategy, it planted enough of a seed of doubt that my would-be jumpers also changed their minds and climbed back to the roadway. The truth is, I had no idea whether or not those thirty-two had changed their minds or not. In the case of one of the suicidal males, I promised him that before taking him in for assessment, I would have a drink with him. Once in custody

I escorted him to a restaurant on Davie Street, where we each had a beer, which was interrupted when the duty officer attended the location and requested an explanation.

While I enjoy solving serious problems, I didn't see myself in the role of a hostage negotiator formally attached to the Emergency Response Team, so when the opportunity presented itself to join, I didn't take it. For the same reason I let my IED (improvised explosive device) credentials lapse. I didn't want be defined as the VPD's "go-to guy" for explosives. With the credentials comes a notation on the daily duty sheet that you are the resident expert and that designation results in you being assigned to every associated incident. I just didn't want my work-life disrupted by being summoned to the scene of every suspicious package or barricaded man.

What does a policeman do when it's really slow in his area? For Crowther and I the answer was to cross the boundary into Team 35's area where the provincial government operated a methadone clinic, and check drug addicts. One day we were in Team 35 territory, westbound on 8th Avenue near Quebec Street, approaching a large parking lot to our north, when we saw five drug addicts doing a death march toward us. The one in front had his head down, an apparent captive, his movements apparently being controlled by the addict directly behind him. The three others were just following. We saw each other at the same time. They stopped, and it was like the graveyard scene in *The Good, the Bad and the Ugly*, with the gunfighters Blondie, Tuco and Angel Eyes staring each other down before committing to action. I floored the gas pedal and we rocketed through the parking lot. There was a momentary hesitation, then the fellow in the front ran toward us, the addict behind him tossed down a double-barrelled shotgun, then he and his buddies scattered westbound. We caught the victim and the fellow who had been carrying the shotgun, but the others escaped. This was the last chapter in another drug debt gone bad.

I have many theories about policing. One of these relates to why criminals who don't hesitate to shoot each other are much less likely to shoot at the police. The theory goes something like this: In western Canada, we have criminals still free in society who have pages and pages of information detailing their criminal convictions because we have the most liberal judges in the civilized world, judges who are incapable of dealing with these repeat offenders who, in a sane world, would never be released from prison. (Not all of our judges, just the vast majority.)

Elsewhere in Canada—and only recently in Vancouver— the definition of a chronic offender was a person who has five criminal convictions in a year. In Vancouver there were so many offenders included in this category that dealing with them was unworkable. Now, to fit the chronic-offender classification in Vancouver the person must have twelve criminal convictions in a year. The Vancouver Police Board was recently told that sixty of these chronic offenders have seventy-five convictions or more, twenty-six have one hundred or more convictions, and the worst four have one hundred fifty convictions or more. So the positive spin on this situation is that criminals generally avoid engaging with the police in violent interaction where injury or death might result, because there is so little consequence when they are caught and convicted.

Liberal judges are not a new phenomenon on the West Coast. When later in my career I was assigned to the

Provincial Unsolved Homicide Unit, the Vancouver Police Historical Society asked me to review the evidence in the murder of Constable Ernest Sargent in 1927 in an effort to understand why the person who did it was charged but not convicted. My review concluded that Constable Sargent was murdered while walking the beat at 11th Avenue and Alder, probably by a notorious criminal named Leong Chung. The statement of the hospitalized and dying constable was weak in that he was unable to describe accurately the number of times he had fired his weapon (he thought three when in fact the number was six) and his positive ID of the suspect in a nine-person photo lineup was tainted because detectives had days earlier shown him a picture of the suspect.

Nonetheless, Chung was arrested and at two different jails admitted the murder of Sargent to two different snitches. The first judge cautioned the jury about the danger of believing the testimony of jailhouse rats but, being guided by case law, he allowed the testimony to be weighed. A conviction followed, then an appeal. The Appellate Court judge excluded the testimony of the jailhouse informants and Chung was ultimately found not guilty.

And now to the fastest confession ever obtained. The undercover RCMP member made his initial approach toward the murder suspect with the request to participate in some shady, but risk-free undertaking for some quick cash. The suspect looked over at him and said, "I don't know if you want to get involved with me, man. I killed a guy a few years ago and the cops are still all over me." The suspect was assured that his previous malfeasance wouldn't be a problem.

A Case of Best-laid Plans

A woman in her late eighties lived alone in her family home on 12th Avenue just east of Victoria Drive. Her son had moved to the suburbs and visited frequently, but she wanted to maintain her independence in her own home. Recognizing that she was frail, she had set up a system with her next-door neighbour. Every morning she would lift up the shade in her kitchen, and this would be a signal to the neighbour that all was well. When the shade wasn't lifted one Friday morning, the neighbour thought, "Oh, she has probably just forgotten," but didn't take any action to confirm that theory. But on Saturday the shade was still down and the neighbour called the police.

I was the acting corporal that morning and as Crowther and I rolled up to the scene, so did another constable and a female reserve officer whose day job was practicing medicine. At the time, Crowther and I took turns kicking in doors, which is pretty much the most fun a police officer can have. It was his turn. The neighbour showed up at the door and told us that the woman's son was on his way and would be on-site with a key in about twenty minutes.

I looked over at Crowther and said, "Kick it in."

The neighbour said, "But he'll be here in twenty minutes!"

Crowther gave me the look that said, "We are just going in to find a body so there's really no hurry."

I told Crowther, "Kick it in now, or I'll kick it in, and this one still counts as your turn."

That old door just exploded in splinters from the frame. I went in first, checking the lower rooms, expecting to find a corpse, but as I went up the stairs, I heard a weak voice calling, "Police, help! Police!" The woman had fallen down between the kitchen table and wall and was unable to extricate herself. Our reserve doctor and I helped the woman up, and she asked, "Why didn't they call you yesterday? The shade was down."

Traffic Division, 1979–81

After about three years of patrolling District Three I was ready for a change. I applied for a transfer to the Coordinated Law Enforcement Unit (CLEU), a provincially funded, integrated team responsible for the investigation of organized crime. When Crowther heard about my application, he urged me to apply instead to the Traffic Enforcement Unit as he had. I couldn't imagine two entities more diametrically opposed than these two divisions. "Come on," he said. "We'll ride those beautiful Harleys! It will be great and we won't have to take any more reports." Crowther had ridden bikes before he came onto the job. I was thinking that the only time I had ever ridden a motorcycle was when a friend lent me a Yamaha 250 that I promptly rode into a ditch near Tannery Road in Surrey.

Fast-forward six months and I was sitting in the personnel inspector's office to talk about my transfer. "I can see that you have applied both for CLEU and the Traffic Division. As it happens, we have openings coming up in both. Where do you want to go?"

I chose Traffic because I thought it would be a lot more fun, and two weeks later I was being fitted for custom-made Wellington-style motorcycle boots.

Motorcycle Training

In 1979 Vancouver's police motorcycle training was done in-house on the grounds of the Pacific National Exhibition in East Vancouver. Eight new members of the Traffic Division arrived for training; along with Crowther, they included two of my academy classmates, Dan Dureau and Christopher Shore. We had all joined the force as nineteen-year-olds. When we were ushered toward a row of intimidating 1200cc Harley-Davidson motorcycles, I asked the instructor, "Where are the smaller bikes that we are going to train on?"

"These are the bikes we train with," he said. "Pick one and get on it."

We started by learning how to coordinate clutch and brake movements and stopping and starting from a straight line. Then cones were set up, and we practiced riding in circles that got tighter and tighter as the course progressed. At the end of the two-week-long course, we headed over to the government facility off Willingdon Avenue in Burnaby, where we all passed the test and received our Class 6 motorcycle licences.

Junior members of the squad were assigned the oldest bikes. In that era Harley-Davidson had been bought up by a recreational equipment manufacturer where quality control was so poor that when the bikes were displayed new in the showroom, sales personnel left sheets of cardboard under the engines so the dripping oil wouldn't stain the floor. So not only did we have the oldest bikes, they were also the worst motorcycles Harley-Davidson ever produced. I chose to work

Cruising northbound on Marshall Street towards Trout Lake on my police Harley-Davidson 1200. These bikes were so poorly made that you could never be sure you would be able to start the engine again after turning it off.

in the northwest sector of the city because traffic congestion there was so bad that I knew I would routinely be the first officer at the scene of a crime. But when I rode out of the Cordova Street garage to begin my shift, rather than ride west to my assigned sector, I would ride south toward the motorcycle repair shop at Manitoba Street and Marine Drive because by the time I arrived there, something on the bike would have broken and needed fixing.

The purpose of having a Traffic Division is to move traffic safely through the city, and that mandate is fulfilled by punishing those who refuse to drive safely. And yes, we did have a ticket quota: fifteen tickets per ten-hour shift. The four of us routinely wrote thirty tickets each shift, and this took three or four hours of focused effort. The rest of our time was spent riding through the sector, showing the flag, doing informal enforcement, crime prevention and covering calls.

Our sergeant was Derek Edwards, a large, powerful man, and at one meeting he became completely incensed at those constables who consistently refused to meet our ticket quota or any other reasonable work standard. Frank Nordel, attempting to justify his own lack of productivity, stood up and expounded on the importance of writing quality tickets, not just a quantity of them. "You should be able to write two to three quality tickets in a shift," he said, suggesting that to write more would be counterproductive. Edwards admonished him, saying that two to three tickets was not going to cut it, and he walked out, completely frustrated by the demonstrated lack of work ethic. I developed my own rule about writing tickets: leave the humans alone. So regular taxpayers got warnings. Scrotes, drunks, criminals and gangsters got tickets. And I've maintained that rule for more than thirty-four years of policing.

Over the Christmas seasons we in the Traffic Division participated in the drinking driver program. We would take out cars and set up roadblocks or cruise the Downtown Eastside looking for drunk drivers. When we made an arrest, we would summon the BAT Mobile (blood alcohol testing unit) and it would arrive with the breathalyzers to process the case. This van was quite cosy inside, having a fridge, soft seats and a sink, and on cold winter nights, in this warm living room setting with its comfortable seats and friends telling stories, what could be more pleasant?

While it was not unheard of in that era to enjoy a warming drink on a cold night, most understood the limits while on the job. Nordel did not. One cold night our crew was working perimeter control on a movie set when one of the production staff approached Sergeant Edwards. He pointed to Nordel, who appeared to be struggling to keep his balance, and said, "Listen, I got nothing against you guys having a drink or two, but that guy is so shit-faced he can't even stand up." I thought, thank God, somebody is finally going to do something about this idiot. Nordel was driven home to sober up. The next day we huddled around the Traffic desk, awaiting Nordel's arrival because Edwards was ready to kill him, but Nordel never showed up for that shift. Or the next shift. He didn't bother showing up for the whole week. When he finally returned to work, Edward's fury had subsided. Nordel blamed the incident on the flu and booked off on paid sick leave.

But the most irritating part of Nordel's personality was his arrogance. Once, when we were standing beside our bikes in Stanley Park, he told us how his class (one of the last classes to have come out of the Vancouver Academy) used to run around the seawall as part of the fitness program and how in those days the academy was a lot tougher than it is now. I looked up and down at his pear-shaped body and offered, "It couldn't have been that tough. You made it."

One time four of us were awaiting the arrival of a wagon for a slobbering drunk that Nordel had arrested. As the wagon driver filled out the paperwork, Nordel told us how he had made his big arrest. As he talked, the drunk edged farther and farther away and then finally spun around and ran off down the lane. While Nordel hesitated as if he couldn't understand how something like this could happen, I said, "Hey Frank, your prisoner is escaping!" Nordel headed off in his riding boots, clompety-clomping after the desperado. And yes, he did catch him.

One weekday I was riding alone in the downtown core at about noon when a call came about a bank robbery a short distance away. Traffic was in gridlock, so I rode my bike up onto the sidewalk and was the first on scene. Over the course of time, bank procedures regarding teller protection, limiting cash on hand and quality surveillance recordings have meant that, these days, a bank is pretty much one of the last places a smart criminal would rob, but in those days there was a real cachet associated with bank robbers. They were at the top of the criminal food chain. In this case, I spoke to the victim, who was still in a state of shock, and I was given suspect details that fit half the men walking in the downtown core. Frustrated, I said, "Okay, what unique thing could you tell me about this guy that, if I walked outside right now, would let me pick him out of the crowd?" The teller thought for a moment, came out of the haze and said, "Oh. Well, he was walking with a really pronounced limp . . . almost like he needed a cane. And he wouldn't be walking anyway because he got into a cab right out in front of the bank." I broadcast the information, and because of the traffic chaos, the suspect was arrested a few blocks away. That really reinforced what I was learning about victims and the information they can provide: never assume that a victim is in shock and can offer only weak information. Always assume the victim has good, accurate information and keep asking until he or she gives it to you.

Welcome to Vancouver

One evening when I was riding alone, I set up radar in Stanley Park, where the only winners of a speeding ticket were motorists caught doubling the limit. Just as I was about to pack up, I looked to the northwest to see the sky quickly turning dark. It was like a blackout curtain was being drawn across the sky from the North Shore Mountains, and I began loading up my gear as quickly as I could. The rain started and it was so heavy that it bounced off the asphalt right back up to my knees. As I was about to get on the Harley, a beautiful Rolls-Royce Silver Dawn pulled in behind me and the driver waved at me through the window. I walked over and spoke to a woman in her sixties, who looked over to her husband in the passenger seat, who appeared to be about forty years older than she was. She was wearing a huge rock on her finger and very expensive clothes. She said, "We're from California and we're lost. Can you tell us how to get to the Bayshore Inn?" I figured they were going to get lost in that downpour and said, "No, I can't. But you can follow me and I'll take you there." I turned on the emergency lights and delivered them to the breezeway of the Bayshore Inn as the rain thundered down in a biblical deluge. The doorman at the Bayshore must have thought I was escorting royalty to the hotel and the front desk had forgotten to give him the memo, but I think I left those folks with a pretty good impression of Vancouver.

On another occasion I pulled over a car full of tourists beside the Hudson's Bay Store on Seymour Street for a minor infraction. The car had California plates and the driver seemed confused as she alternated between fumbling in the glove box for the insurance papers and fumbling in her purse for her driver's licence. I decided to cut the exercise short because she was taking far too long finding her documents and ultimately I was just going to give her a warning anyway. I asked her name, which she readily provided. The conversation that followed went something like this:

Me: "And Carol, where are you from?"

Carol: "Hwhy?"

Me: "Well, it's a requirement of Canadian law that you tell me where you are from, so let's try it again. Where do you live?"

Carol: "Hwhy?"

Me: "Okay, Carol, I think I've explained the legal requirements clearly enough. You are required to tell me where you live."

Carol: "Hwhy?"

Me: "I'm going to give you a few minutes to reconsider your position, then a paddy wagon is going to make an illegal left turn onto Seymour Street—just like you did—then pull up beside us, load you up and take you to jail."

I left Carol for a few minutes and returned to find that she had started to cry. Finally locating her driver's licence, she presented it to me. Carol and her passengers were from Honolulu, Hwhy.

Shiny Side Down

I started keeping track of how many times I dropped my bike. The first happened when one of the senior members of the squad had let me borrow his brand new 1980 Kawasaki KZ1000, which was the fastest production bike on the market. This first accident was fairly mundane and involved my dropping the bike while westbound on First Avenue just west of Boundary Road. Nothing spectacular, no injuries. The bike just came out from under me and I was left standing in the middle of the road watching it scraping along on its crash bars as it continued down the road without me. The senior constable was surprisingly understanding.

Number Two happened when I was working alone in Stanley Park and two drug addicts passed me driving an old pickup truck—stolen, of course. A female was driving with a

This Kawasaki 1000 was the fastest production bike model on the road. Ironically, while the Harley had no kick-starter and frequently needed it, the Kawasaki had one but never did.

male passenger. I put on the lights and siren and pulled them over just past Brockton Oval on Park Drive. When they pulled over and stopped, I angled my bike away from the curb (just like they taught us at VPD motorcycle school) and started to get off, keeping my eye on the two in the truck. But as soon as the truck stopped, the driver and passenger began trying to switch places—I suppose this was so the male could play the role of gentleman and take the rap for driving the stolen truck. While they were going through this acrobatic manoeuvre, one of them hit the gearshift, putting the truck into reverse. As it slowly rolled over my motorcycle, I stepped away like a matador avoiding the bull. It was evident that the driver had not meant to drive over me, but had the two of them simply driven away at that point, I would have had no way of pursuing. I walked up to the driver's door, tapped on the window with the barrel of my pistol and said, "Get out."

Number Three happened when I was in the curb lane eastbound on Robson Street approaching Burrard, and a vehicle in the lane beside me changed lanes right into me. Having pretty fair reflexes, I rode the bike up onto the sidewalk and crashed it into a mailbox. The driver got a ticket. His defence was that I was the one who had an accident, and that it had nothing to do with him.

Number Four occurred as I was southbound on Granville Street near Nelson and heard a commotion—doors slamming, tires squealing—just to the west. I realized a vehicle was rocketing southbound down the lane at a high rate of speed, so I rode west across a parking lot to intercept it. When the car finally came into view, I saw it veer toward a scruffy-looking, long-haired character standing about fifteen yards in front of me in an apparent attempt to hit him. The intended target raised a pistol and fired three times as the car swerved past, barely missing him and continuing down the lane. I dropped the bike and drew my revolver, pointing it at the shooter, who had his back to me. I called out, "City Police! Drop that gun," and the man turned toward me with his hands at his sides. I warned him two more times, thinking that he appeared to be in a state of shock. Finally calming, he yelled, "RCMP! RCMP!" Again I ordered him to drop his gun, which he refused to do. Just then I noticed a Vancouver Drug Squad sergeant running toward me from the south. He was a friend of mine and a fellow member of the Vancouver Police Pistol Team. He called out, "Wayne, he's RCMP!" before going over to relieve the shooter of his firearm. When I returned to the station, the story was all over. The corporal asked, "Why didn't you shoot him?" The first reason was that when the shooter opened fire, he crouched and used a two-handed grip on the pistol. The average drug addict would not normally have that kind of training and discipline, so it clicked immediately that something was wrong with the scene. The second reason was that I was a pretty good shot, and I had drawn and aimed at a shooter who had his gun at his side; at point-blank range I was confident that I had control of the situation. Besides, he had already missed the driver of the car with his three shots.

For Number Five I pulled over a westbound vehicle on Georgia Street, directly across from the Hudson's Bay, for a routine traffic stop. It was rush hour so there were well over seventy-five people on the north sidewalk waiting for the bus, and now they were all watching me. The car stopped without incident, I put down the kickstand of the Harley and leaned it over. That's when the kickstand snapped, and the bike went onto its side with me on it. I got up, dusted myself off, walked up to the driver and told him to get lost. I rode the Harley back to the city works yard, where I leaned it up against a wall to await repair.

I had a few more accidents while in Traffic Division. Fortunately, in this instance, I was driving a car, not a bike. Westbound on Cordova in the curb lane, I was stopped at a red light beside a tractor-trailer. With the light still red, the driver of the tractor suddenly decided to make a right turn, crushing the police car against a power pole. As I climbed over Crowther, I hit the lights and siren before the two of us spilled onto the sidewalk. This driver actually advised me that the accident was my fault because I was in his blind spot.

Although the members of Traffic Division ride our bikes in the sun, rain and sleet, we don't ride in the snow. In one of the few blinding snowstorms Vancouver has ever had, Dan Dureau and I were westbound on Cordova Street in one of the big Traffic Division battlewagons. Dureau was driving, and it was slim pickings for tickets when we noticed a vehicle driving toward us with one headlight on. Dureau pulled a U-turn behind it and put on the lights and siren. The vehicle pulled over without incident but stopped right in the middle of an intersection where the northbound traffic would be approaching down a very steep hill. I got out and approached the driver, an Asian male who apparently spoke no English.

His wife was the passenger. I told the driver several times to pull forward because any northbound vehicle would never be able to stop in the ice and slush. Exasperated, Dureau got back into the police car and drove it up the hill, where he meant to block northbound traffic that could slide down the hill and collide with our stopped offender. At the top of the hill he turned the police car to face us, but it began skating down the hill toward us in an uncontrollable slide. Standing at the driver's door, I told the fellow, "You have to move right now." No response as he continued to search in his glovebox for the car's paperwork. Just seconds before the collision, Dureau hit his lights, which caused the two in the car to look to their right as the police car crashed into the passenger side door and blew the car right through the intersection.

As the ambulance arrived, the female passenger alleged she had been blinded and had to be carried from the wreck. As the ambulance drove away with the woman in the back, the husband, recognizing that he had made a mistake in not feigning injury like his wife, ran in the snow behind the departing ambulance, yelling, "Wait! Wait! I'm hurt, too."

Throughout my career I would periodically remind Dureau about the incident: "Remember that Chinese woman you crippled on Cordova Street?" His response was, "She was Vietnamese."

Back in the early 1980s the VPD had its own Parking Enforcement Squad, police officers who rode small, three-wheeled Cushman motorcycles all over the city and wrote parking tickets. (Since that time the squad has been replaced by a civilian detail that focuses on bylaw enforcement.) This Parking Enforcement Squad didn't work Sundays, so early one Sunday morning, Dan Dureau, Christopher Shore and I booked out the Cushmans and rode them over to the PNE,

53

where we chased each other all over the grounds in these ridiculous motorized clown cars. Then we lined up three abreast on Hastings Street at Boundary Road. We raced the engines (all thirty-five horsepower), and when the light changed, we floored it. I was approaching the crest of the hill at Renfrew Street when I smelled something burning. I careened over to the curb, stopped and got out to see that the brakes had somehow locked, causing a fire that had now spread to the fibreglass undercarriage. We borrowed a fire extinguisher from a taxi, put out the fire and had the burned-out hulk towed back to the station. In my defence, I have to say that at the time there was no actual rule or directive or policy that forbade members to book out the Cushmans. That policy was enacted immediately thereafter.

Traffic Division is either in your blood or it isn't, and after six months Crowther bailed out. I had discovered that Traffic wasn't in my blood either, but I couldn't, in good conscience, leave the division after I had gone through all of the training. In fact, I just found the job to be too mundane, and I didn't like the continuous negativity associated with giving out tickets all day long. In 1980 I applied for an instructor's position at the British Columbia Police Academy. My wife and I were expecting a child, and I thought that the academy instructor's position would offer some dayshift stability as well as giving me licence to shoot endless amounts of free ammunition from the widest possible variety of firearms.

There aren't many secrets around the police department, and when I received a letter from the Justice Institute of British Columbia in the departmental mail, my Traffic squad knew what was up. As I opened the letter, "Dog Balls," one of the more vocal members of the crew, said, "Is that your Thanks-but-no-thanks letter?" I read through the document and responded, "No, it's my Thanks-but-thanks letter." And I passed my letter of acceptance to the Academy around to the incredulous non-believers.

Police Academy Instructor, 1981–83

It's Not a Bullet, It's a Cartridge
I started work as a firearms instructor at the Justice Institute in the first week of January 1981. That someone would pay me to shoot and to teach others to shoot was a dream come true. Even now I enjoy shooting and a good day is one spent at the range. As a former police chief once commented, "A bad day at the range is better than the best day at the office."

My son Chris was born on January 26 of that year. I couldn't have been happier.

Corporal Bill James was the other firearms instructor. His background was with Vancouver's Emergency Response Team (who we were mandated to train), while mine was with Police Combat Shooting. An RCMP staff sergeant headed the Firearms Section, and the director of the academy itself was Chris Jones, a retired RCMP member. Though the RCMP didn't participate in municipal training, they were qualified to give it. As the criteria for employment at the academy was only that you had to have police officer status, any Canadian police officer could apply for a job there. My experience was that the mix of instructors was a good thing. I think that in my pre-police college days, when the VPD ran its own academy, having only Vancouver instructors offered a more limited view of policing. But at the Justice Institute, I got to know some pretty outstanding people, including Larry Young, a corporal who taught fitness training at the Justice Institute, who died in 1987 in a shootout with an armed gunman.

Teaching at the academy offered the opportunity to shoot a wide range of firearms. This one was a 9-mm. MAC-10 submachine gun.

At that time we were teaching instinctive shooting at metal targets at close range. To demonstrate how effective the technique was, I would lie on my back seven metres from the metal plate, extend my arms over my shoulder and—without using the sights—shoot a very small group of rounds into the centre of the target. Twenty-five years after I left the academy, when I was working a historical homicide file, I phoned the Delta Police Department to get some information. After I identified myself to the desk sergeant, there was a pause before he asked, "Is this the same Wayne Cope who taught me shooting at the Academy and shot bulls' eyes while lying on his back by just pointing at the target?" I responded, "Yeah, that's me." I had no problem getting the information I needed for that file.

One morning I gave a demonstration to the class followed by some practice shooting. The recruits left for lunch and when they came back, they were told to return to the outdoor firing line, where the instructors would meet them shortly. As I came out to the line, Jim Bellevue, one of the more gregarious members of the class, was lying on his back with his gun out, pointing it at the target. When he saw me standing over him, he said, "The gun's not loaded." But even with an unloaded gun, what he was doing was strictly against range rules. As he rolled over to get up, I said, "If I thought that gun was loaded, I would have you terminated if it was the last thing I ever did." I followed up with a few additional comments, and let it go at that.

More than twenty years later I was in an elevator full of police officers at 312 Main Street, the police station annex, when I looked over to see Bellevue staring at me.

He said, "You couldn't do it, could you?"

"What was that?"

He responded, "You said you were going to get me fired if it was the last thing you ever did. You couldn't do it, could you?"

I then realized that as he rolled over to get up, he hadn't heard me preface my threat with: "If I thought that gun was loaded." If our discourse in the elevator had been more civil, I would have straightened him out, but given his manner, I didn't see the need to clarify what was actually said. As it turned out, a short time later Bellevue was fired (resigned under duress) because of an unrelated incident. I briefly considered meeting with him to let him know that I had gotten him fired after all, that it had just taken longer than anticipated.

One of my pet peeves at the Justice Institute was instructors who talked down to their students. My position was that, by sheer odds, half of the students were smarter than their instructors. The only reason these students didn't lash out when being berated was because of their fear of the consequences.

One of the perks of teaching at the Academy was that instructors were allowed to travel to Ottawa to take training courses, usually once a year. I took the mandatory Instructional Techniques Course and then signed up for a Crisis Management Trainers Course. I had to have approval from the academy's director, Chris Jones (who also happened to be a friend of mine), and he asked me why I wanted to take the course. "I don't really think it's your style," he said. "It teaches how to teach other people how to talk suicidal people off bridges." I said, "Four reasons: it's in Ottawa, it's in the spring, it's three weeks long, and there is no final examination." And away I went.

One consequence of the enormous amount of hiring that was going on at that time was that very junior constables were being promoted to the rank of corporal without much experience. In my view, this is a mistake virtually every time. I was on the elevator with one of the more obnoxious promotional errors when one of the other occupants, pointing to the new chrome chevrons on the novice corporal's collar, asked, "What do your friends have to say about your promotion?" He responded, "I don't need friends now that I have these." A veteran constable in the back of the elevator looked over and said, "Keep talking, kid, and I'll shove those stripes right up your ass." The junior corporal considered his options, then got off the elevator at the next floor.

Occasionally the academy would run double classes, which meant all hands on deck at the shooting and driving ranges, and even our staff sergeant would attend to assist with the teaching. Because of the scheduling at these times, unless we were running overlapping training blocks, when recruits attended the range, the other academy instructors had free days. The only significant assistance ever offered was from Larry Young. He was an Emergency Response Team Member who really enjoyed spending the day at the range doing recruit training, so he would volunteer when he had an "open day." One of the most enjoyable training sessions was a week-long course in May 1985, when Bill James, Larry Young and I ran an Emergency Response Team training course at the Chilliwack Military Base and the Port Coquitlam Hunting and Fishing Club on Burke Mountain. The training for this course was skills based with final tests involving scenario evaluation. I didn't have the background to offer anything other than general advice on tactics, so my focus was on marksmanship, and from that time on, Larry dubbed me "Billy-Bob Swilley" because he said I reminded him of a "good old boy" Southern sheriff. Whenever we would pass, even in the slightest proximity, I would hear a high-pitched, "Beely, Beely-Bob . . ."

About a year after I became a full-time academy instructor, Dan Dureau and Christopher Shore were transferred there as well to teach traffic studies. Shore had been in three major motorcycle accidents while with the Traffic Division. Each of them happened exactly the same way: he was riding straight through an intersection on a green light when a vehicle coming the opposite way turned in front of him. The last accident was the most serious, and he was hospitalized for a long time.

Tiger, Tiger

Whenever we did training at the outdoor range, we would hang out a sign indicating that the place was closed for the day. Frequently people would drive by and, seeing all the

A simulated hostage rescue at the Chilliwack Armed Forces Base in 1985. Corporal Larry Young was carrying an experimental prototype .12-gauge shotgun while I held a more conventional .223-calibre Colt AR-15.

cars, assume the range was open and the sign was wrong. We would normally shoo them away, but on one occasion I opened the door and recognized Tiger Williams standing on the porch. At the time, Tiger was a Vancouver Canucks forward and a renowned enforcer who still holds the NHL record with more than 4,400 penalty minutes. He said, "Oh, you're closed" and was about to walk away when I invited him in and asked what he was shooting. When he produced a Smith & Wesson .357 Magnum revolver, I told him that he could shoot while James delivered a lecture inside to the recruits. I watched Tiger for a short while and noted that, despite the fact he was shooting a Magnum pistol that kicked like a mule, he showed no sign of a flinch. I guessed that he was used to ignoring pain. When I commented he had shot a really good target, he challenged me to a shooting match. He presented the challenge so earnestly that I could see the competitive spirit that made him such a great hockey player.

I said, "You can't win."

He bristled back, "Oh, why is that?"

"Two reasons," I said. "One, I've seen you shoot, and two, I do this for a living." And three, I thought but didn't say out loud, I don't want to lose a shooting match to an amateur in front of all of these recruits. No, I didn't take up the challenge.

Fraternizing

I don't condone fraternization between male academy instructors and female recruits, but a few instructors (and recruits) were notorious for this. It was so bad that at one point Chris Jones, the director of the Academy, set out a policy that office doors would remain open when instructors were inside. He confided to me, "Wayne, I knew something was up when they started using cologne. Cologne at a police academy, can you believe it?"

One time a particularly attractive female recruit (who I knew was dating one of my fellow instructors) came into my office while I was at my desk revising a manual. She said, "You're a friend of [no, I'm not going to name him], aren't you?"

Without really looking up from my paperwork, I responded, "Yes, I am."

"He's really young and he has been divorced twice," she said. "He seems to have gone through a lot of relationships with a lot of women. So I'm wondering," she mused, "if he's picking the wrong women . . . or is it him?"

I moved the papers off to one side, put my pen down, looked her straight in the eye and said, "It's him."

"Really?" she said.

"Yes, really," I responded. In the end, though, the two moved in together and were a couple for some time.

Whenever one of the recruit classes graduated, we all went down to the legendary Police Athletic Club at 190 Alexander Street to celebrate. The Vancouver Police Union had purchased the whole building at the north foot of Main Street, and the sixth floor had become an exclusive police drinking establishment.

My door card for the Police Athletic Club. Originally a small private storefront club located in the 200 block of Main Street, it relocated to the top floor of 190 Alexander Street when the Police Union purchased that building.

On one of these occasions it was late when I headed to the elevator. The doors opened and one of the graduating female recruits was in the embrace of one of the instructors. I gave her the combination head shake and eye roll. She responded by saying, "Oh, lighten up. You could be next."

Beat Cop, 1983–85

After two years teaching at the Academy, I was ready for a change. While in-service and Emergency Response Team training was challenging, most of the work I did was with new recruits, and I could only give the "It's not a bullet, it's a cartridge" lecture so many times before I was ready to jump off my own bridge.

In 1983 I was transferred to Vancouver's Granville Street beat in District One. I was in my element. Virtually all of the crime in that area (or the city, for that matter) was committed by drug addicts, and the Granville Mall was ground zero for the city's trafficking activity. My partner was Cal Roberts, and we were like carnivores surveying the Serengeti for our next prey. We conducted every kind of surveillance there was—on foot, in cars, from inside stores, from abandoned premises, from rooftops—and we got great results.

In later years when I became a sergeant in charge of one of Vancouver's drug squads, I testified in court that I had made hundreds and hundreds of drug arrests, probably more than a thousand. An incredulous defence counsel quizzed me, "A thousand? Would you like to run that out for me?" I said, "Sure. First of all, what constitutes an arrest? It's when you take somebody into custody and search him. When you are walking the beat, it would be an extraordinary thing not to do that three or four times a shift. Second, in the course of a shift, if we didn't process at least one person for drug trafficking, I would have considered that shift a failure and hope to make up for it the next day. Let's say there are 200 working days in the course of a year; that easily adds up to 600 arrests a year. I walked the beat for three years, so I have made well over a thousand drug arrests."

My partner, drinking at the old Police Athletic Club, pauses in conversation, turns his head and hurls, then returns to the topic without missing a beat.

Me: "Did you just throw up?"

My partner: "Oh, you noticed that, did you?"

Don't Make Eye Contact

When we worked afternoon shift, we would request permission to dress in plainclothes in order to conduct "buy and busts." This would give us the opportunity to wear outlandish disguises to make undercover drug purchases from the same crooks we spent the rest of the time harassing while we were in uniform. It was a lot of fun seeing who could wear the most outrageous outfit or hairstyle and still make a purchase. One of my favourite outfits was a shiny, light-brown, double-breasted, leather trench coat, which I wore at night with dark sunglasses, my hair slicked back and a smoldering cigarette in my hand. I was going for the psychotic "Taxi Driver" effect.

While assigned to the Granville Mall, we ran week-long buy-and-bust drug operations, and wore outrageous outfits to make purchases.

The drill was to purchase drugs throughout the week, then do a roundup on the last day of the shift. Drug traffickers aren't that smart, but they do have a certain animal wariness about them. I had bought drugs off of a trafficker one day and the next day was participating in a sweep to bust him when I noticed him loitering in the middle of the 800 block of Granville Street. Ideally when an undercover drug purchase is made, a uniformed officer will be called in later to make a positive identification, but sometimes this is not possible because traffickers often sell and then move on. In this case, to avoid arrest and charge, this fellow would merely have to leave the area to remain anonymous, so I was determined to get him. I approached him with my head down and didn't look up until I was about six or seven metres away from him. Well, I wasn't a very good actor, because he caught on. He spun around and started to sprint. I dived after him and began grabbing onto his loose clothing, which unravelled like toilet paper off a spool. I finally grabbed a piece of clothing that didn't rip off and spun him around into a wall. Only it wasn't a wall. It was a plate glass window about two and half metres tall by three metres across that exploded around us. I pulled him away from the shards and put him in handcuffs.

Months later I gave evidence in federal court about the case. I don't know why, but in the course of my testimony I didn't mention breaking the window. The judge was relatively bored by the proceedings and appeared to be working on his grocery list or maybe a crossword puzzle. The evidence went surprisingly well, and I was just thinking that it was a slam dunk, when the first words out of the defence counsel's mouth were, "Constable Cope, is it true that the first thing you did when you met with my client was to throw him through a plate glass window?"

Uh-oh, I thought, and noticed that the judge was now wide awake, glaring at me and acutely anticipating my response. The look on his face said that my answer had better be good.

"Tell me why you didn't mention this in your evidence?" he said.

Here we go, I thought. "Your Honour, the reason I didn't mention it in my evidence was because I didn't want to prejudice the court against the accused."

"Really?" the judge said.

"Your honour," I said, "the first thing the accused did when I placed him under arrest was try to escape. We struggled and he fell against the window. I saved him from injury by pulling him away from the falling glass. Since this is a charge of drug trafficking, I didn't think that it would be fair to the accused to discuss how he had also attempted to escape lawful custody in the course of the arrest."

The defence was deflated. The judge smiled and gave me a "well done" nod.

I was one of the few police officers among my colleagues who enjoyed testifying in court, and as I was usually involved in the type of policing that resulted in a lot of arrests, I spent considerable time on the witness stand. As long as I spent an appropriate amount of time refreshing my memory with the facts of the case, I found that testifying was much the same as telling an interesting story—without the pleasure of poetic licence and embellishment. However, I was routinely in court two or three times a week, and I found it very hard to function when that attendance was made in addition to an afternoon or night shift. But police officers on afternoon and night shifts testify so frequently that an abandoned part of the city jail was outfitted with mattresses and sheets so officers could catch a few hours of sleep between their day in court and returning to work.

I remember testifying in court about another case, on a later occasion.

Defence counsel: "Sergeant Cope, is it true that my client stopped behind one of your vehicles at a red light, then you rammed your car into the rear of my client's car, locking it between your car and the unmarked police car in front? And is it true that when he got out and refused to comply quickly enough, he was knocked to the ground?"

Me: "Your Honour, I don't remember the specifics of this incident, but what defence counsel has just described is exactly what should have happened—a classic Tactical Vehicle Takedown, a TVT. It's part of the STAR training that all of our members receive." I considered telling the court that I had been one of the authors of the STAR manual, but I decided against it.

Hizzoner Constable Steve Barrie

One of our best undercover buyers was Steven Barrie, who was a friend of my brother's and had also attended Langara's Criminal Justice Program. I had known Steve since he was a teenager and he still looked so young it was incomprehensible to sellers that he could be a cop. He would speed past them on his skateboard, spin it up on two wheels, catch it and then ask what they were selling. One evening we were working together in a patrol car and were approaching Gastown westbound when we received a call. It had just rained and the cobblestones of the one-way street were so wet and slippery that when Steve hit the gas, we did an unintentional but perfect 180-degree turn, resulting in us travelling 60 km/h, in the wrong direction, on Water Street. As we eased to a stop, I put on the lights, no siren, and we slowly drove off down a side street. No accident, no harm, no foul.

Later, when I was a corporal assigned to the public information counter, I worked with Steve again. A typical fraudster came in to report that his welfare money had been stolen and that he needed a police file number so it could be replaced by the ministry. Barrie quizzed him across the counter. "So they took all your money, then?"

"Yes, they did," the liar explained.

"Everything?" Barrie countered.

"Everything," said the fellow emphatically.

"Then you won't mind if I have a look?" Barrie asked.

Taken aback, the fellow grunted, "No, I don't care," not believing a policeman would actually make the effort to do a full investigation.

But Barrie vaulted the counter in an instant and patted the fellow down to find eight hundred dollars in his jacket pocket. No file number was forthcoming for this fellow and his money was tagged as evidence of a fraud.

Another time, Barrie was driving through the prairies on a lonely stretch of Highway 1 when he looked over to the oncoming lanes, where a Mountie was being pummelled by some cretin he had stopped. Barrie pulled over, ran across the highway and subdued the attacker. RCMP management was thankful and wrote to Vancouver's chief constable, recommending that Barrie get a Chief Constable's Commendation, a very prestigious award. The chief wrote back thanking the RCMP for their kind comments but noting that, since Barrie already had his Chief Constable's Commendation for the year, he wouldn't be getting another one.

Barrie was the only policeman I ever met who would routinely get letters from the judiciary to the police department commenting on the excellence of his evidence. He was one of the finest police officers I ever worked with and had a distinguished career. Later he became a tactical member of the Emergency Response Team and then left the department to attend UBC's law school. He became a respected lawyer and prosecutor and now sits as a provincial court judge.

Going Postal

One morning I was called to a Canada Post branch office in Yaletown, where a disgruntled employee had pulled a knife on his co-workers and was making threats. The area was contained and tactical units had just started pulling up when I noticed an Emergency Response Team (ERT) officer beside me loading a tear gas canister into a thirty-seven-millimetre Smith & Wesson tear-gas gun. This was a shoulder-fired, Al Capone–era weapon that the department still had in use at that time, and it was capable of firing an assortment of projectiles, including flechettes (resembling large model rockets) that were designed to deliver tear-gas powder through a door into a residence. When loaded with a riot canister, like the one being put into it at this scene, the gun delivers about twelve ounces of tear-gas powder with an effective range of about twenty metres. As the drama unfolded, the knife-wielding suspect stepped outside the office to speak to police, whereupon the staff slammed and locked the door behind him. So the scene ended with knife-man, the ERT with his cannon and me in a standoff about five metres from each other. Finally I looked at the ERT member and said, "Oh, go ahead." BOOM! The powder, which was designed for a riotous crowd, hit Mr. Postman full in the face, which became completely engulfed by the volume of powder that had hit him. He blinked twice through two little holes in the red dust and then fell over.

Blue Canaries

In the old days canaries were taken into the mines because they were so sensitive to poisonous gases, and when they keeled over, it served as a warning to the miners that it was probably a very good time to leave the area. Because the members of the police department are always out on patrol, they usually get to the scene of casualties, collisions, fires and all manner of similar disasters before other first responders. As a result, the fire department calls police officers "blue canaries" because, being first on the scene of a disaster such as a fire, they take in noxious fumes without a self-contained breathing apparatus (SCBA), which is similar to scuba equipment without the underwater component.

On one occasion my partner and I were westbound on Hastings Street, heading toward the Main Street police station, when we saw smoke billowing out of the front doors and windows of the Balmoral Hotel. This hotel was notorious for drug and criminal activity, but there were also a number of elderly and infirm people living there. We radioed in and called for assistance, and as I parked on the sidewalk in order to keep the roadway clear for other first responders, I could hear sirens coming from both the fire and police stations. With help on the way, we entered the lobby as people streamed out onto the street. Keeping low to avoid the smoke, we headed up to the top floor, where we began banging on and then kicking open doors and escorting residents to the stairs. We had cleared the top three floors and were heading down the stairs when we met firemen coming up. Knowing the hotel would shortly be completely clear, my partner and I headed for the street, where we hacked and coughed and spewed up all the toxins we had just inhaled. Then, still barely able to breathe, we got into our police car and headed for St. Paul's Hospital, where we were given oxygen, treated and released. That's when I mentioned to my partner that they would probably have to demolish the Balmoral because of the damage. He said, "Are you serious? A few coats of paint and some new carpet and that place will be up and running again in a couple of weeks." He was right.

Several months later a number of constables were called into the inspector's office for a meeting. When I asked the corporal what was up, he advised me that these were the officers who had rescued all of the residents of the Balmoral, and the inspector was awarding them commendations. Apparently a roll call had been done at the scene of the fire, and a list had been drawn up of all of the heroes present, many of whom hadn't even entered the hotel. My partner and I, of course, were not in attendance to add our names to the list because we were at the hospital being treated for smoke inhalation. When I suggested that our exclusion from the presentation of awards was inherently unfair, the corporal said that the Commendation Award ship had already sailed and we were not destined to be aboard.

Rule Britannia!

Coal Harbour, which sits on the edge of Stanley Park, is one of the most idyllic maritime settings in the world. It is home base for commuter service companies that employ every manner of amphibious aircraft, from old de Havilland Beavers to modern Twin Otter seaplanes, and it is a favourite destination for the seagoing rich and famous.

In 1983 one of the visitors to the harbour was the Queen's royal yacht, the HMY *Britannia*, and I was determined to get on board for a tour. By virtue of the fact that my partner, Cal, was an officer with Canada's Naval Reserve, he had an invitation to an evening social event at HMCS *Discovery* in Stanley Park, and I would be his plus-one. As we were on duty that night, he couldn't participate in the formalities, but he did drop by in uniform to check out the after-party.

"Find me the Officer of the Day," I told Cal, "the person in command of that boat, and get me an introduction." I could see the look on his face. He was obviously thinking, Oh no, here we go! But he located Lieutenant Commander Wilkinson, the ship's executive officer, and introduced me. We had a friendly chat, and then I asked if we could have a tour of the *Britannia*. Wilkinson was polite but very firm. "No, this is the Queen's own vessel and certainly not open for tours. If it were any other ship but this one, there would be a possibility, but in this case, sorry, but absolutely not."

I accepted the rejection. Cal schmoozed a bit longer and then I told him it was about time to head out. He said, "What's the rush?" And I told him that we had to get our ship's tour in before our sergeant noticed that we were missing. A short time later we presented ourselves to the armed guards on the gangplank of the *Britannia*. The young non-commissioned officer in his bright white, starchy uniform asked, "Yes sir, what can I help you with?"

I said, "I was just over at your Officer's Reception at HMCS *Discovery* and spoke to Lieutenant Commander Wilkinson who said that, if I dropped by here, I could come onto the ship for a quick tour."

The NCO looked at me quizzically. "Wilkinson said that?"

"Yes, he did," I said.

The NCO turned and beckoned me to follow one of the sailors up the gangway. I was surprised to find that there were many scantily clad young women on board, none of whom appeared to be in the navy. At one point during our informal tour a warning was yelled, and all of these cavorting young women ran for cover, diving to get out of sight. When a false alarm was called, they were immediately back in view.

For a ship that doesn't give tours, they ran a pretty good one. Everything was spic and span on this yacht that doubled as a hospital ship when not in the Queen's personal service. It actually had a canteen where I purchased a plaque and a crystal beer mug, both of which sported the *Britannia* logo. She was, without a doubt, the prettiest ship I have ever been on.

Booty from our tour of Her Majesty's yacht *Britannia.*

Detective Cope, 1985–88

Back in the early 1980s the first level of promotion in the Vancouver Police Department, as in the military, was to the rank of non-commissioned officer or NCO. There were three levels of NCO at that time: corporal, sergeant and staff sergeant.

A corporal, who was the first level of supervisor and the junior NCO, would be second in command of a ten- or twelve-man squad and act as sergeant in the senior NCO's absence. An advantage of having a junior NCO in charge of a team was that it allowed the sergeant to spend more time supervising on the road, while the corporal shared the office paperwork. Another plus was that, if the corporal turned out to be a screw-up, ending his career at the junior NCO level would limit the damage he could wreak on the department. Having said that, I also have to say that some of the finest officers I have known never expressed any interest in promotion to NCO or the officer ranks.

The rank of corporal had an equivalent rank of detective, though a detective usually did not have officers under his command (except in Strike Force), and the rank was more of a job description with a 15 percent pay increase over that of constable. Some of our finest detectives only ever wanted to be detectives and had no wish to command police officers in the field.

The role of sergeant was to offer guidance and direction, to prepare others for leadership positions, to take command of dangerous situations and to enforce policy and discipline. With the exception of those in charge of Internal Affairs (Professional Standards), Strike Force and Historical Homicide, sergeants did not conduct criminal investigations. The staff sergeant was the highest-ranking NCO and acted as an administrative liaison officer between commissioned officers and all other ranks. Generally, constables were paid 100 to 105 percent of base rate, corporals were paid 115 percent of base and sergeants were paid 125 to 130 percent of base rate, depending on seniority and excluding overtime.

The first level of commissioned officer was in those days—and remains today—inspector; above inspector is superintendent, deputy chief constable and then chief constable. The police union has no voice in the selection of commissioned officers because, at that level, they are management. So the police board selects the chief constable, and his team of commissioned officers is selected by a panel. From Don Winterton to Jim Chu, I worked for seven chief constables, and over the course of my career I have found that decisions made by the chief constable dealt with the big picture and rarely had an impact on the street level work I was involved in. As a front-line officer and later an NCO, I really had no interest in involving myself in the cerebral aspects of police management, but I have to say that for the most part, Vancouver has always enjoyed progressive, forward-thinking leadership, and its policy and procedures are frequently used as a model by other metropolitan police departments.

In 1985 the VPD eliminated the corporal, detective and staff sergeant ranks. Constables could now realize a corporal's wage by passing tests, taking courses and accruing seniority. Detective was no longer a rank but was now a job description that could be assigned to a constable. The sergeant was now all alone, working with no support for supervision and paperwork. It was a coup for the police union, but a mistake for the police department. The rank of staff sergeant has since been reinstated.

Our inspector observes an RCMP officer in the joint forces drug squad unit showing off a new semi-automatic pistol to one of the Vancouver detectives by quickly racking the slide back and forth.

The inspector: "I have been watching you, and I don't think that you are handling that weapon in a safe manner. I'd like you to put it away."

RCMP: "Yes sir." Rack, rack . . . BOOM!

The Idiot Factor

In the VPD the average size of a squad led by an NCO is nine, eight of which are positive, well meaning, relatively conscientious professionals who truly want to offer service to the community. One of the nine is a (pick one or more) lazy, stupid, incompetent, insubordinate, scheming malcontent whose presence actually reduces the effectiveness of the policing unit with which he or she is associated. In an organization like the VPD, where reputation precedes one, the vied-for positions in specialty squads have fewer idiots because they are screened out, while less desirable positions in unpopular squads have more. This screening process as one advances through the ranks reduces the Idiot Factor to about one in twelve.

With the RCMP, the Idiot Factor is seven, meaning that one Mountie in seven is an idiot, and the promotional process within the RCMP actually increases the Idiot Factor to one in five. This is because the promotional process and dynamic within the RCMP is so easily manipulated by schemers, bullshit artists and carpet trolls. One of the main problems is that officers compete for promotion and transfer to specific jobs rather than just applying for promotion. As desirable jobs come with specific requirements relating to mandatory qualifications, one of the many possible manipulations is to have a friend or mentor of higher rank write up a job description so specific that only the desired candidate will qualify.

The VPD is much less likely to see the system gamed because of the transparency of the promotional process and the protections offered by union oversight. My personal experience has been that when the department is tagged by a legitimate grievance, the manager responsible will be held accountable. So grievances against the VPD are few and far between.

Still on the topic of idiots, I was on a Major Case Management Supervisors course run by the RCMP in which the instructor ran out a case study and asked for comments regarding training and development. The scenario was that officers with a warrant had searched a property relating to a homicide investigation. Subsequent to the investigation, they learned of a secondary residence that had been involved and proceeded to search that place without a warrant. The question was: "What action, if any, should be taken regarding these officers?" It was pretty much unanimous that the investigators needed counselling, training, educating, etc. so it wouldn't happen again. But one of the RCMP officers, who supervised a larger metropolitan contingent of general investigators, said that he wouldn't take any action, and the instructor asked him, "Why not?"

He answered, "If I could ever get those lazy, useless malingerers to get off their worthless asses and leave the office to do anything that even resembled police work, I could never chastise them for making a mistake."

Another interesting issue that was discussed at length on this course was the effect of "groupthink" on investigators. It's something that I have seen many times—dissenting opinions being discouraged and even ridiculed in the course of an investigation. As part of the course, a recommendation was made that early on in any investigation a "contrarian" should be appointed for the specific purpose of offering an opposing opinion. I think that this is a really good idea, but in any investigation I have been involved in, I have always acted as a contrarian without formal appointment. I always picture myself standing in front of a jury, defending a course of action or a shaky warrant, and then I try to visualize every single weakness that exists in the way the investigation is being conducted.

The Public Information Counter, 1985–86

There are number of supervisory jobs in the Vancouver Police Department that nobody wants to do, and assignment to one of these areas is known as "doing your inside time." These assignments include working at the public information counter, the city jail and the Communication Centre, and in my day new NCOs could expect to spend between six months and a year working at these assignments before being transferred to uniform duty. Some newly promoted supervisors seemed to avoid these assignments through fortuitous timing, political influence or both. I was never one of those chosen ones. For me, the promotional handshake was always the prelude to an "inside time" assignment. In 1985 as a newly minted corporal, I was assigned to the public information counter with the added caution that I would actually be spending most of my time assigned to the city jail.

The public information counter at that time was one of the worst posts in the city to work. Unlike the sanitized (and civilianized) environment that exists today, the counter then was truly open to the public, with only a short counter separating staff from people who felt compelled to walk into the police station to report crime rather than have the police attend their homes. Drug addicts and drunks used to flake out on the wooden benches and do who-knows-what in the public washroom. The phone rang endlessly with endlessly idiotic questions from endlessly idiotic people. To this day when a phone rings, I have a primal urge to smash it into the wall. And whenever we got a break from dealing with the idiots on the phone, we dealt with the idiots who had wandered through the front door, eager to talk to a policeman. My time on the public information counter may have unduly influenced my perspective on people and the questions they ask. Later in life when I delivered lectures I would always encourage the audience to ask questions, but I would add, "I am not one of those people who believe that there is no such thing as stupid questions. There are, in fact, stupid questions, and they are usually asked by stupid people."

Strike Force Detective, 1986–88

When I was promoted to corporal, I had applied for a detective's position with the Strike Force, which focused on targeting and arrest. It had two core mandates. The first: to target high-profile criminals and then embark on a program of surveillance to catch them in the act of committing crimes and subsequently make arrests. Each target became the focus of a project that usually ran for two weeks. The second mandate: to act as Vancouver's problem solver. A kidnapping occurs—call Strike Force. A woman phones in to say that her estranged husband is going to rob a bank this afternoon—call Strike Force. There were two teams within Strike Force, each comprised of one sergeant, two detectives and seven constables. The sergeant oversaw the running of the squad and the two detectives ran the day-to-day surveillance, supervising the work of the constables. All Strike Force personnel were trained in the use of special weapons, as well as in advanced surveillance and arrest techniques.

However, Strike Force also had one detective known as the intelligence coordinator who was supposed to assess information that came to the unit, prioritizing it for action. The reality was that this detective answered the phones and acted as squad secretary while the sergeants decided which files they were going to work on. At that time management couldn't get anybody to act as squad secretary so I was given a choice: take the intelligence coordinator's position for a year and then transfer into one of the Strike Force teams as an

An assignment to Strike Force allowed me the opportunity to grow a beard and long hair.

operational detective for two years or wait for who-knows-how-long while maintaining a holding pattern at the public information counter. I told the staff-development section I had no interest in being the Strike Force receptionist and I stayed at the public information counter. About ten months later I was awarded a detective's position. For a young policeman it truly was the best kind of work to be doing.

In those days Strike Force was a pretty tightly run ship. The sergeant would occasionally come out to play, but for the most part he stayed in the office contemplating the nature of leadership and plotting his next promotion. The two detectives were both Type A personalities who had a tight rein over personnel and operations and acted as "road bosses" to direct the moment-to-moment surveillance activity. All of the team members got along extremely well both on and off the job. At that time I was a pretty avid craps player, and I taught my teammates the game; this was long before bored surveillance personnel could occupy their downtime with Google, Netflix, Facebook and texting.

When I arrived in the Strike Force, another classmate of mine who was now on the unit was about to be promoted and transferred, so I recommended Christopher Shore for his job, and soon we were working together. We grew long hair and beards and wore earrings, and we used to joke that we bought all of our clothes at the Salvation Army, although we got the same clothing allowance as detectives working Homicide or Robbery who were required to wear suits. My most freakish appearance was when I grew my hair far past my shoulders and cultivated a long beard. One weekend I decided to dye both jet black. On Monday morning I got on the elevator at the lowest sub-floor to be joined by my Strike Force crew, who got on the same elevator two floors up. All conversation stopped as they stared at my new look. Finally the silence was broken when one of them said, "For the love of God, isn't somebody going to say something?"

That same week we were doing foot surveillance in the area of 10th Avenue and Clark. I wore a black trench coat down past my knees to reinforce the homicidal effect of the hair, and the only thing missing to complete my outfit was a butcher knife or a hatchet. In the park on the

This was my most psychotic undercover look. It even prompted one of my Strike Force associates to comment, "For the love of god, isn't somebody going to say something?"

southwest corner a woman sat reading on a bench while her child played on the swing set, and as I crossed between her and the child, she looked up, saw me and screamed. Then she ran past me, scooped up her child and escaped westbound.

Generally, our time was spent taking on any two-week project where surveillance would lead to arrest. The simplest of these were breaking and entering investigations. Then in January 1986 the law regarding prostitution changed, making it illegal to communicate in a public place for purposes of prostitution, and we added arrests of this kind to our caseloads. At that time my personal car was a 1973 Dodge Dart with a broken muffler; I had bought it from my old traffic corporal for $1,200. As my backup team hovered in the background, I would pull into the curb lane and cruise up beside a hooker—who no doubt believed that no policeman would ever be caught dead in such a piece of junk—and collect evidence of public solicitation. But although the new laws relating to prostitution were fairly straightforward, our judiciary showed no interest in taking action against these fallen flowers. So once we established what the limits of the law were, we discontinued using the Strike Force as an extension of the Vice Unit.

One of our best Strike Force files involved a case where two Vancouver Roma factions had gone to war with each other. One of their minor skirmishes culminated with a member of one group being kidnapped by the other, and the second to last scene in the kidnapping drama saw the victim being held down by several of the rival members, one of them a female. The victim's pants were taken off, and the woman pulled on his scrotum with one hand and brandished a knife with the other, about to administer castration. Sparked by an adrenaline surge, the victim spun out of the melee and escaped by diving through a window.

Normally the Roma culture demands that no mention of this would ever be made to the police, but in this case the victim thought the rival group had stepped over the line and reported their identities and location to the police. The last scene of the performance: my Strike Force team smashed through the door of an apartment and confronted the gang. We could see the fear and shock on their faces as they scrambled for the shotguns and other weapons that were within easy arm's reach, but they stopped immediately when they heard "Police, don't move!" and saw our clearly marked raid jackets. I remember seeing the relief on their faces. It was clear that they were thinking, "We are in luck! It's only the police!"

That scenario resonated with me throughout my later career, particularly during my three years with the Drug Squad, where I took part in hundreds of warrant executions.

Whenever we smashed in a door and made entry, I always ensured that the first person through the door (usually me) called out clearly, "Police! We have a warrant!" About the last thing in the world I wanted was to shoot some weapon-brandishing drug trafficker who thought he was protecting his property against a drug rip-off.

One of the most straightforward cases I dealt with while I was with the Strike Force involved a man attempting to sell a derringer at the Balmoral Hotel on East Hastings Street. The information was pretty good: he was an older fellow seated in the middle of the bar and the pistol was in his boot. Since I was heading back to the station and was in the area, I volunteered to deal with the call. The plan couldn't have been simpler: I would go in, make an assessment and ultimately confront the suspect. Patrol units would wait outside, give me five minutes and then come in to assist with the arrest.

I entered and took a seat about two metres from the target, who was exactly as described and looked out of place in a bar that catered to the Downtown Eastside. I watched him for a few minutes, then walked over with badge in one hand, gun in the other, and very quietly told him he was under arrest. I told him I knew that he had a gun in his boot and that I was not going to disarm him now. I ordered him to stand up and walk slowly to the entry hall (outside the beer parlour) where I would handcuff him. I also told him that if he ran or reached for his gun, I would fire my revolver six times as fast as I could pull the trigger into the small of his back. He offered no resistance and was taken into custody by patrol units who arrived as planned. A loaded .45 calibre derringer was recovered from his boot.

When I arrived in Strike Force, all the surveillance training for our members was performed by the RCMP's surveillance unit known as "Special O," a unit that had no mandate to arrest and even included some civilian members. But about midway through my tour of duty with Strike Force, the RCMP decided that Special O would no longer do this training, so in company with Sergeant Harold Thomas and Detective Jeffrey Morrison, I sat down with the members of Special O for a week and, with their blessing, co-opted every surveillance idea they had ever conceived of and then added a number that they hadn't. I think my best contribution was to advise our team of plagiarists that the most important aspect of the exercise was to ensure that the training package had a cool acronym. And that is how the STAR manual (an acronym for Surveillance Tactics and Resources) was born. As far as I know, it's still used as a training resource today.

I had been in Strike Force for about a year and a half when I had an interview with Staff Sergeant Norm McWhinney. He was an old-school policeman, a complete authoritarian who believed you were either on his team or you were the enemy. Until this point McWhinney and I had a fairly good relationship, but now he advised me that there was going to be a new staffing policy in Strike Force: since management still couldn't get anybody to apply for the intelligence coordinator's position, the operational detectives were going to be rotated through that job for a period of six months each, and I would have the honour of taking the first six-month stint on that job. I told him that I had already turned the job down and that the rejection had condemned me to extra months working at the public information counter. I said that I wasn't capable of sitting at a desk for ten hours a day listening to the phone ring, because every time it did I felt like smashing it into the wall. I used every argument that I could think of, but when I was finished and started to rise, he said, "Wayne, I don't hear you saying that you are going to quit over this, so you will start here at shift change."

I sat back down, looked him straight in the eye and said, "If you think that is what's going to happen, then I haven't articulated my position clearly enough to you."

He seemed astounded and requested that I spend the weekend thinking about it.

I said, "We can do that, but you have your answer now."

When I left the office, Detective Shore was called in. He came out a few minutes later, shocked. "Did you just tell the staff sergeant to go fuck himself?" he asked.

I responded, "I wouldn't have put it exactly that way."

"Wayne, we have to straighten this out," he said and went back into the office. When Shore returned, he said, "He'll reduce it to three months. Three months for you and three months for me. You have to do this."

I agreed and became the squad secretary for three months. But though I had compromised, I figured that this was strike one against me.

When I arrived for duty at the intelligence coordinator's desk, McWhinney mentioned that he had just approved the outgoing detective (Morrison, who had been my co-author for the STAR course) for a commendation for the work he had done in that position. I suppose this was an effort to motivate and enlighten me as to how important secretarial work was. When this disclosure met with an uncontrollable eye-roll on my part, he asked what was wrong. I told him that unless Morrison had performed some heroic act on his lunch hour, it was hard to believe that he accomplished anything of value sitting behind that desk for the past six months. I am pretty sure this was strike two against me.

Strike three came when Norm asked if he could accompany me and a group of friends on a hunting trip. I tried to be as pleasant as possible, explaining that my buddies and I had hunted together for years, and I just couldn't bring an outsider. He then offered to come along as camp cook. I said no, I just couldn't do it. From that moment forward I was the enemy. A short time later McWhinney was promoted and transferred, but before he left, he took the time to mention to the incoming staff sergeant and my squad sergeant that as far as the next Sergeant's Promotional Competition was concerned, they could put a red line through Detective Cope's application. The new staff sergeant in Strike Force assured me that the promotional situation would right itself in the future, but he couldn't interfere with McWhinney's decision on that year's competition.

McWhinney's claim to fame in later years was being a principal plotter in a coup d'état against our chief constable, an officer who had once been his friend. He was pretty much universally despised for his role in that piece of departmental history.

The Dog Squad, 1988–91

Me, attempting to improve the spelling and grammar on a constable's Dog Bite Report: "You write that your dog chased the suspect down the lane and cornered him in the Elk Cove. Is that where the elk go to vacation in the wintertime?"

I was offered a third year in Strike Force and declined, deciding instead to apply for the training supervisor's position with the Dog Squad because it offered an opportunity to do a completely different type of policing. I had never been a dog master, which normally would have vetoed my application to that squad, but Dave Thurston, the sergeant in charge of the unit, had an open mind. I had three things going for me: no corporal or detective with Dog Squad experience had applied for the job, the corporal who was in that job now wanted a job in Strike Force and the sergeant had heard that I had outstanding supervisory skills. (I suspect this glowing endorsement regarding my supervisory skills had been made by the incumbent dog-training corporal who wanted to swap for my job in Strike Force.) There was also the fact that Thurston had been an instructor at the old academy, and I think our common backgrounds worked in my favour. Even more in common was that he had put himself through university by lifeguarding at the same beaches and pools that I had, though this was years before I had arrived on that scene. He once told me how he had been manning a lifeguard skiff at New Brighton Beach on June 17, 1958, when the Second Narrows Bridge—then under construction—had collapsed, killing nineteen ironworkers. He rowed to the scene of the carnage but lamented that he had been unable to save anyone.

After I got over my surprise that my application for the Dog Squad had been accepted, I immediately began preparing myself for my upcoming training. First, I would have to take the three-month-long basic dog master training program, then I would have to work in the field as a dog master before taking over as the trainer. Ultimately I would have to present myself to the provincial court for certification as an expert dog-training supervisor. The BC Supreme Court would grant that certification.

In 1988 the Vancouver Police Dog Squad was comprised of twelve handlers and their dogs, supervised by a corporal and a sergeant. The dogs are principally used for tracking criminals, but they can be used to locate people hiding in any defined space, including warehouses, boats and residences. They can also be used to attack armed criminals, locate drugs or find lost property. The VPD Dog Squad provided twenty-four-hour coverage of the city, and because of overlapping shifts, we were also available to cover serious calls at shift change. I certainly had the best-looking dog on the squad. PD (police dog) Wolfe was a purebred, long-haired German shepherd that had been donated to the police department by a supportive, public-minded citizen.

Police dogs are extremely well treated. They are assigned to dog masters who keep them at their homes. Vancouver City employees pour a cement pad on the dog master's property, and on this they build a large wooden shed to serve as a doghouse. Beside it they prepare a long gravel run and enclose it in a chain-link fence so that the dog has a large area in which to run free. The department provides all dog food and pays for any veterinary treatment required. Whenever I made purchases related to care and feeding, I usually just selected the best quality.

A purebred German shepherd, PD Wolfe was the most photogenic of Vancouver's police service dogs (in my opinion, anyway).

On February 21, 1988, I started the VPD's dog master training course, which is such a highly regarded program that it routinely accepts trainees from American police departments. Classes have between six and eight dog master teams and begin with general socialization. The dogs are usually between ten months and a year and a half old. Pre-training can involve obedience to simple commands such as sit, stay and come, but it is preferred that they are not trained any further than this so that the methods of training all of them are identical.

Socialization involves teaching the dogs to move in proximity to each other without displaying aggression. On the first day of training, they snap and lunge, requiring their

PD Wolfe won a silver medal at the 1989 International Police Service Dog Competition held in Delta, BC.

masters to use collars and leashes on them; on graduation day, the dogs lie down in a line, then each in turn walks that line off leash, stepping over each prone dog without reaction from either dog. Other training includes tracking, searching for property and aggression.

Wolfe was not a particularly aggressive dog, but he was an outstanding tracker and in 1989 won the silver medal for the property search scenario at the International Dog Trials held in Delta, BC. Sergeant Thurston's dog, on the other hand, was known as the Alligator. On one occasion a suspect had been trapped in a locked yard but refused to give up. Thurston heaved his dog up and over the six-foot fence to make the capture, whereupon the Alligator clamped onto the suspect, who screamed and screamed as the constabulary broke their way into the locked compound.

I Don't Even Like Dogs

Policemen are a lot like soldiers, many of whom are not happy unless they are complaining about something, and I had been with the squad for about three months when I heard the usual griping and whining coming from the report writing room. The gripe of the month was about arbitrary transfers, and how many of the changes didn't seem to make any sense. I was not participating in the argument, but as I walked past the group, I commented, "I don't know why they sent me here. I don't even like dogs." There was stunned silence and I just kept walking. (I was just trying to torque them up. As a point of clarification, I really do like dogs.)

Occasionally I would take Wolfe out on patrol and offer up my services as a district supervisor. I would speak to the area NCO by phone first and obtain agreement for two reasons. First, even though I was offering a favour, the job was really his, and taking over required consent, regardless of my seniority. Second, in practical terms, you really shouldn't have two supervisors working in the same area; the other personnel need to know that there is only one person in charge.

Sometimes I would take a ride-along passenger in the police car, and once I took my sister-in-law's cousin. We had finished a few hours of patrol when I decided to head back to the office. On the way I stopped to pick up my dinner from a Kentucky Fried Chicken—some fries and three pieces of chicken in a cardboard box—but on the way back to the office there was a family-trouble call, and the unit there asked for cover. Since we were close by, I stopped to help, advising the cousin to wait in the car, as I didn't anticipate that the call would take very long. I left my dinner on the front seat, and as I exited the car, I slammed the Plexiglas window that sealed Wolfe into the back. I was in the apartment building for about five minutes dealing with the call, but as I walked down the front stairs, I could see that Wolfe had slid the Plexiglas panel open, and his head was fully inside the KFC bag. My passenger had sidled over until he was up against the window, not wanting to get between Wolfe and my dinner. I yelled and ran toward the police car. Wolfe lifted his head out of the bag, gulped something down and put his head back into the bag. As I opened the door, he lifted his head out of the bag again, this time with a drumstick hanging out of his mouth, before he retreated back to his lair. I grabbed the bag and checked the contents. He had emptied it of all the chicken, leaving only the fries intact. My passenger said, "I just didn't know what to do, but I sure didn't want to get between him and that chicken."

One of my favourite Dog Squad experiences concerned a constable who was involved in a chase after a stolen vehicle in Stanley Park. I was on patrol on the west side and listened to the radio exchange as I drove toward the scene. The car thief had crashed the vehicle into the woods, jumped out and headed for the trees. The dog master deployed his dog, who bounded after the driver, but twenty minutes later, although search quadrants had been set up, the crook was still on the loose and the dog was missing in action.

Then one of the containment units came on the air and broadcast: "Constable Harper, we have your dog. He's just come out of the woods near Park Drive over near the rose garden. We'll hold onto him until you get here."

Harper: "Thanks, I'll be right there."

Containment unit: "Hold on! The crook has just come out of the brambles and is running northbound on Park Drive."

Harper: "Point the dog at the guy who is running away and yell, 'Take him!' Then release the dog."

Response: "Okay." Then moments later the officer keyed the mike so that we could all hear the sound of screaming. Another outstanding dog case concluded successfully.

Thurston was an excellent dog trainer. He was very knowledgeable and gave an animated and enthusiastic presentation. He had a lot of service behind him, but at one point he had quit the job, zeroing his pension plan. His plan now was to stay with the Dog Squad until retirement, maximizing his pensionable service, but once I had taken over training, he had an even better gig worked out for himself. As the Dog Squad was an independent unit, he was pretty much allowed to run it autonomously as long as the job got done. He was living in Langley at this time, and over the course of one winter his drill was to arrive after rush hour, about 9:45 a.m., and be gone before rush hour started again around 4:30 p.m. It was a combination of a modified dayshift and the I'll-be-working-from-home-today scenario. One week his driveway froze over with ice, and he didn't come in at all. Fortunately, the squad still had supervisory oversight as I was usually involved in training and pretty much worked a steady afternoon shift.

Then one day I was called down to the inspector's office at 312 Main Street. The staff sergeant was very solemn as the inspector broached the subject. "Wayne, we understand that you have spent the last few months on some kind of abbreviated dayshift, and at one point your driveway in Langley was iced up and you didn't come in to work at all. Can you tell us what's going on down there?"

Oh brother, I thought, some scheming little rat has surfaced, but he's bungled his report. "Your information is completely wrong," I said. "If you check the duty sheets, you will see that I have spent most of the last six months on afternoon shift. As well, I live in Coquitlam—not Langley—and have never missed a shift because of the weather, nor have I ever missed a shift that wasn't properly documented. I can't imagine where this type of nonsense has come from."

Not surprisingly, the duo failed to offer up their source, but surprised by the assertiveness of my rebuttal, they transitioned quickly to other business.

One evening there was a call about a prowler breaking into a ground floor suite where a young girl was in bed. She phoned 9-1-1 and gave a play-by-play account of the suspect first being in the yard, then working on her bedroom window with a pry bar. Units were quickly set up a block away to contain the area and await the arrival of a dog master who would swoop in for the arrest. As the dog master advised radio that he was four minutes away, the girl whispered to the dispatcher that the suspect had the window partially opened and was trying to enter. At that point I directed the dispatcher to have the patrol units put on their lights and sirens and attend the victim's location. Seeing the perfect "dog case" slip between his fingers, the dog master advised that he was only two minutes away. The dispatcher repeated this information. I advised, "This is an order. I am ordering the containment units to put on their lights and sirens and move directly to the scene. Code 3, lights and sirens." The would-be victim later told us that the suspect was just stepping into the suite when he heard the sirens, climbed out of the window and ran. To my knowledge he was never caught, but I count this as one of the best decisions I ever made as a police supervisor—though I got a lot of heat for it from the squad members.

Dawna

One of my motives in transferring to work as a dog-training supervisor for a few years had been to introduce the stability of structured shifts into my life, but it was too little, too late. As happens far too often in the policing profession, the years of overtime, shift work and court attendance all contributed to the breakup of my marriage. In the spring of 1990 I became a single father living with an eight-year-old son. A few months later I spoke to one of my co-workers on the Dog Squad, whose wife worked in the VPD's Communication Centre, to ask him about Dawna, a police dispatcher whom I had seen but never met. After determining that she was single, I asked that he set up a double date for him and his wife, Dawna and me.

Back when I had been walking the beat on Granville Street, Dawna's father had been the inspector in charge of my team and now was the superintendent in charge of the Dog Squad. He later went on to become the Chief of Police. We had always got on very well, but the last time a police officer had expressed an interest in his daughter, the aspiring suitor had received a single .38 calibre cartridge in the departmental mail.

Dawna and I dated for about a year with no bullets in the mail, and we were married in October 1991. We are still very happy, and Dawna still works with the Vancouver Police Department as a senior director.

Gun Slinger

The first gift I got my new wife was a Browning lever-action rifle; I wanted to serve fair warning what she was in for. Many police officers have no experience with firearms, and other than the weapons they are issued by the department, they have little proficiency with or understanding of the workings of other pistols, rifles or shotguns. Other officers like me, far fewer in number, are avid hunters and fishermen who collect rods, reels, fishing gear, knives, shotguns, flintlocks, percussion locks, pistols, rifles, cannons, swords, spearguns and anything else related to outdoor life.

While much is said about how our American cousins have far too easy access to guns and how this has contributed to a gun culture, the reality is that with two exceptions there is not much difference between our two countries regarding access to weapons. The first of these exceptions relates to carry permits for handguns; there are virtually no circumstances that would allow a Canadian citizen to carry a handgun on his or her person. The second exception is Canada's general prohibition of automatic weapons (machine guns and submachine guns). Canada also has some specific prohibitions relating to the barrel and overall lengths of firearms.

Prospective firearms owners in Canada must be federally vetted and approved prior to being allowed any access to guns. Handguns require one kind of permit; rifles and shotguns require another. To buy or possess a handgun, a purchaser must be a member of a range and be able to vocalize a good reason for wanting to own a gun; being a collector, shooter or hunter are acceptable reasons for wanting to own a firearm, while self-defence or personal protection are not. Handguns may only be transported to and from a range or to and from other locations designated on the permit. The rules relating to the transport of rifles and shotguns are far less restrictive, and there is nothing wrong with, say, taking a properly secured firearm to a friend's house to show him the newest acquisition. Given that firearms permits are pre-approved, there is no waiting time or numerical restriction relating to the purchase of rifles and shotguns, nor is there any upper limit on the amount of ammunition one may possess. (In case you are thinking of purchasing a cannon or mortar, the restriction on the volume that one can own of black powder—the explosive cannon propellant—is twelve kilograms!)

I have always maintained the largest spectrum of licences and transport permits. One very quiet Sunday I arrived at the Dog Squad office with a newly purchased Winchester bolt-action rifle in .375 Holland & Holland Express calibre. I had bought a new scope and hadn't had time at home to mount it onto this new elephant gun, so I had brought it into work, where I could "bore sight" it. I was in the office when one of the dog masters came in and said, "Check the radio! There is a black bear running amok over at the PNE." I turned on the radio, and sure enough a bear was being chased through the neighbourhoods just east of the Pacific National Exhibition grounds. This was probably fine at 7 a.m. but wouldn't be as amusing after Playland opened at 10.

I headed over there to learn that McWhinney was coordinating operations. The bear had run into the blackberry brambles just north of the east parking lot. Feigning the proper respect for his authority, I advised McWhinney that in the event that he wanted to have the bear shot—and there were many opportunities as the bear dodged between the brambles and the parking lot—I happened to have an elephant gun on my front seat. He gave me a why-doesn't-that-surprise-me look and said that we would await the arrival of a Conservation Department officer who would deal with the bear. Forty-five minutes later the bear was still in the brambles when the Conservation fellow arrived to guarantee McWhinney that he would kill the bear with one shot, which would be safely made at close quarters with his rifle (which was much less powerful than mine). McWhinney gave him his blessing and he went into the brambles after the bear while we all watched. By the shifting of the brambles we could watch the CO's progress following the movements of the bear, which was always about ten metres in front of him. Move and countermove, the dance went on for about fifteen minutes, but the distance between them never closed. Finally the CO emerged, his arms covered in blood where the brambles had cut him, and offered up Plan B.

We got the fire department to bring out one of their pump trucks and had them spray the southern margin of the brambles, back and forth and closer and closer to the bear, the idea being that the animal would be forced to flee the torrent by escaping northbound onto Cassiar Street. The CO and I awaited the arrival of the aquaphobic bear from a position just north of the brambles, but there was no immediate result. Then suddenly the huge black bear exploded out of the undergrowth and up the hillside toward us. The CO fired off three quick rounds from point blank range, and the bear tumbled backward down the hill into a large furry ball. The CO slung his rifle, then he and I slowly approached the carcass. But as he leaned over the body, the bear roared to life, spewing pink bloody foam and striking out with his claws, just missing the CO's face. Not having time to unsling his rifle, he reacted with a fast draw of his pistol and fired three more rounds into the bear's chest. Now completely perforated, the bear fell back into the ditch, finally dead. I looked over to the CO and commented quietly, "Nice shootin', Tex, but what happened to the one-shot theory?"

Hunting Rabbits

In April 1990 real estate developer and philanthropist Earl Lohn told female friend Melissa Nurani that he wished to end their acquaintanceship. Melissa, understandably distraught, went into Hunter's Sporting Goods on Kingsway at Gladstone and told the staff there that she wanted to buy a double-barrelled shotgun. Asked if she was planning on hunting some rabbits, she answered, "No, something a bit bigger."

On April 26 I was driving westbound on Broadway close to Main Street when Nurani and her double-barrelled shotgun walked through the ground floor of 1665 West Broadway. Employees in the reception area phoned Lohn on the fourth floor to warn him that there might be a problem. He was on the phone taking the call as Nurani came through the door and fired both barrels into his chest. Then she dropped the shotgun and took the stairs down to the third floor, where she was detained by a very large fellow who looked like he might have been a rugby player. The call came through on the radio at about 3:45 p.m., which was the same time as shift change, but I was at the scene moments later and parked my police car on the sidewalk in front of the building. I came through Lohn's office door to find him sitting erect behind his desk. He wore a silk tie, which at the third shirt button down had been blown into a large wound in his chest. The tie exited the wound just below the sternum and continued down to his buckle.

Three hundred years earlier, when the British were involved in colonial expansion, there was a theory that the front-line troops should be issued silk shirts. At the time it was thought that thick, tightly woven silk, being such a hardy material, would capture bullets and not allow them to pass into the body, much like modern bulletproof vests do today.

Looking at how that shotgun blast blew through Lohn's silk tie, I can offer definitive information that the theory was false.

Two doctors who had come from the medical office across the hall stood against the wall to my left. Recognizing that the victim was deceased, I nonetheless went over to him and attempted to take a pulse from the side of his temple.

"He's dead," said one of the doctors.

I said, "I know, but I'm not going to be able to take your word for it."

I called radio and advised that I was with a homicide victim and was told that there were no units available to assist because of the shift change. At this point one of the office workers rushed in through the open door and said, "She's downstairs! They've got her downstairs!" I escorted the doctors out, posted one at the door and told him not to let anyone in, then went down the stairs to find Nurani sitting in a chair against the wall, her passage blocked by the large young man. I arrested her for murder, gave her the legal warnings and put her in handcuffs. Then I asked the fellow who had taken her into custody if he was okay with staying with her. He said that he was, and after I quickly ascertained that he was of good character, I told him, "I am deputizing you a police officer for the City of Vancouver. Hold this woman in custody until relieved of duty by a uniformed constable and allow her to talk to no one." He agreed to do this, and I returned to Lohn's office to secure the scene. It took a long time for backup units to attend.

Guns, Guns, Guns

Whenever policing is discussed, inevitably the conversation turns to the type of guns that are used by various police departments, and why they were chosen. The first gun I ever used was a Smith & Wesson Model 10 revolver in .38 calibre with a narrow barrel and checked walnut grips. These were issued to police reservists who accompanied regular constables out on patrol. The issue holster was made locally by a cobbler on Main Street in south Vancouver. The department had just quit using a cross-draw holster and had adopted one with a flap that was secured by the use of a stud that pushed through the hole like a button on a shirt. This was not a good way to secure a firearm, as the flap was either locked down too tight so the gun had to be extracted using two hands, or the hole was so worn that the flap was forever opening on its own. Later versions saw the introduction of a steel rivet that allowed the holster to pivot so it would lie flat against a vehicle seat. But when chasing a suspect on foot, officers had to keep one hand on their gun so it wouldn't pinwheel off the gun-belt and launch onto the street.

At Oakalla Prison the issue pistol was a .38-calibre Colt revolver that was very similar to the Smith & Wesson in design and capacity (six rounds of ammunition) except that the cylinder revolved clockwise rather than counterclockwise. This is actually a very important distinction that the shooter has to be aware of. In the case of a zombie attack where a single round of ammunition is lying at the shooter's feet, with a Smith & Wesson the officer would open the cylinder and put that round into the one o'clock position (rather than the Colt's eleven o'clock position) and then close the cylinder. As the trigger is pulled, the round at one o'clock rotates counter-clockwise into the twelve o'clock position where it is fired, rather than with the Colt, where the gun would go click, click, click, click, click and then boom.

Most members of my class of recruits were issued brand new Smith & Wesson Model 10 pistols with heavy barrels and custom handgrips to reduce the recoil of the new, more powerful "+P" ammunition. They were the newest, prettiest, most comfortable, most accurate revolvers made. I didn't get one. My battered, old, used pistol was with me for another year before a new shipment of guns arrived. But once I had my bull-barrelled Smith in my hot little hands, I attended the VPD range and spoke to the armourer, who happened to be on the VPD Shooting Team with me. When I left the workshop, the innards of that gun had been jewel polished and the trigger honed to a smooth spur. The pull of the trigger and the hammer movement was as slick as melting ice and ready for the next provincial shooting competition, but the gun still qualified to be certified for the "service pistol" competition because the only work done on it had been completed and approved by a departmental armourer. I wore that gun for almost twenty years, at which time it was replaced by the Beretta 92F. The Beretta company had won a contract with the American military, and because of its advanced features, the pistol was being adopted by many US police departments who felt they were under-gunned when dealing with violent criminals.

By this time the revolver had been obsolete for almost a hundred years. When Bill Miner—Canada's first train robber and the man known for coining the phrase "hands up"—robbed the Canadian Pacific's Imperial Limited in 1906 at Monte Creek, BC, he was carrying a Luger 9-mm semi-automatic pistol. During World War One, American troops were issued .45-calibre semi-automatic Colt pistols. And both of these handguns were vastly superior to the revolvers we were issued in the VPD in 1975. In modern times the only advantage a revolver can offer would be to an assassin who doesn't want to eject empty shell casings (evidence) across a crime scene when he shoots his victim. It is also easier to silence a weapon that has no side ejection of supersonic gas.

Over the years the VPD went from low velocity (800 feet per second) round-nose lead ammunition to a slightly higher velocity (+P) round-nose, then to a higher velocity hollow-point and finally a high velocity, jacketed hollow-point. It is peculiar that, while the Geneva Convention forbids the use of hollow-point ammunition (dum-dum rounds) for use in war, they are almost universally used in policing. But a solid case has been made relative to the stopping power and over-penetration of round-nose (ball) ammunition, so now hollow points are all that we carry.

With a revolver, the gun holds six rounds, and twelve more are issued and carried in speed-loaders or drop-down pouches. When firing a 158-gr bullet, the bullet carries 203 foot-pounds of energy. With the Beretta pistol, the gun holds twelve rounds, one in the chamber and eleven in the magazine. Officers are issued two full magazines, which are carried on the belt. The holster is a high-quality composite design that offers protection from attempts to seize the weapon while still giving the wearer quick access. The gun has no safety but is double action, which means that it cannot be cocked and each trigger pull is a duplicate of the other. With a trigger pull weight of just over ten pounds, it's not likely that the gun is going to go off by mistake.

With other semi-automatic models, the first round is fired with a full trigger pull of ten pounds, with each subsequent round touching off at just under five. Competitive shooters cock the hammer on their pistols for the first round so that each and every round can be touched off with a light five-pound trigger pull. It is thought better to go the safe route and have a heavier trigger than have a more accurate gun that might be inadvertently fired because of a light trigger pull. The Beretta's .40-calibre bullets have a velocity of about 1,200 feet per second and carry 500 foot-pounds of energy, which is almost two and a half times more powerful than the .38. In short, the new pistols are cannons compared to the weapons that we were issued when I first joined the police force. Additionally, with requisite training and certification, constables can now sign out and carry .223-caliber semi-automatic rifles or be outfitted with a 12-gauge shotgun, which must be carried securely in the car trunk. And more recently the SIG Sauer pistol has replaced the Beretta, but it is comparable in style and firepower. These are all good forward-thinking, positive changes that have been made to counter the weapons being carried by violent criminals. Although the Emergency Response Team has always been equipped with appropriate weapons, I never thought that I would see the day that police officers would have such a formidable arsenal at their disposal.

In 2006, when I went to work for the Transit Police, I received one of their standard issue .40-calibre German Glock pistols. At the time I had heard that a friend of mine (the Transit Police firearms instructor) had just taken delivery of a little mechanism that, when installed on the Glock, converted the gun to fully automatic fire. This meant that it would take just one trigger pull to empty the whole magazine. However, fully automatic fire is generally discouraged because in a ten- or fifteen-round burst, usually only the first two rounds are on the target; after that the explosive recoil causes the barrel of the gun to rise uncontrollably off-target.

We arrived at the range with my Glock 27, 40-calibre sub-compact pistol and waited for the Justice Institute staff to finish up with the recruits they were dealing with and go for coffee. As soon as my Transit Police crew and I were alone at last, I had our instructor turn my little baby Glock into a fully automatic pistol. I stepped up to the target with his advice ringing in my ears: "You are really going to have to hold onto it."

I let her rip. I held the gun horizontal for the first three rounds but in the second it took to empty the nine-round magazine, the gun went up and up and pounded the last two slugs into the ceiling. Cement, plywood and drywall rained down on us. I hesitated for a second then yelled, "Quick, find a broom before they get back." When the range staff returned, we were just leaving. They didn't send us a bill for the damage, so either they didn't notice the alterations to the range or decided that they just gave it more character.

The Major Crime Squad, 1991–93

After two years with the Dog Squad, with Thurston's encouragement I entered the promotional competition for sergeant. At that time a promotion was dependent upon the candidate acquiring enough points to achieve a score higher than the scores of other candidates. By far the greatest weight was given to points awarded by the Promotional Round Table, a secretive "star chamber" where the issues discussed stayed in-camera and where all of the officers and NCOs presented their people to determine a competitive score. The most highly thought of candidate scored one hundred points; the most poorly thought of candidate about forty-five. After the Round Table's decision, secondary factors were considered, such as a promotional fitness assessment done by the candidate's immediate supervisor, post-secondary courses completed while on the job, sick leave taken, the Assessment Centre (an independent leadership evaluation program run at the Provincial Justice Institute) and the promotional interview. But with fifty-five promotional points up for grabs at the Round Table (the difference between the best and worst scores), these other factors were virtually irrelevant.

Thurston walked out of the Round Table and met with me right away. "What did you ever do to McWhinney?" he asked. "He hates your guts." I told Thurston that it mostly had to do with a hunting trip I wouldn't take him on.

After my third year with the Dog Squad I attended the inspector's office and told him I was ready for a change. He seemed disappointed. "Actually," he said, "we had planned for Sergeant Thurston to leave and you to stay." I told him I understood but that I was ready for a change and was hoping to transfer to the detective office and try for a position in the Major Crime Squad.

Wolfe retired from the Dog Squad with me. However, he was not really a house dog and not all that smart, and his favourite indoor activity became sprinting down the hallway, leaping over the large plush chair in the living room, crashing into the wall, then shaking it off to take another endless lap. This caused me to return him to his doghouse outside where he had the run of our large backyard.

A short time after he became an outside dog again, our neighbours acquired a large white female poodle. Our fence being only a metre and a half high, he was over it in one bound. The neighbours called to say that they enjoyed Wolfe's company but wanted to make sure that it was okay with me that he was spending so much time at their house, visiting his new girlfriend. He enjoyed his last years migrating between the two houses, putting in less and less time in his wooden doghouse and more and more time sleeping at the foot of the neighbours' bed.

Getaway Van

My appointment to the North Detective Office came almost immediately after my request for a transfer. It was not the position I had been hoping for, as the North Detective Office was an entry-level detective office that conducted follow-up investigations for all manner of mundane crimes in the city. Still, there were some good cases. One of the better ones involved the robbery of Nick's Spaghetti House, at the time one of Vancouver's hallmark Italian restaurants, situated on Commercial Drive in Vancouver's Little Italy. On May 8, 1991, two men wearing motorcycle helmets and brandishing weapons robbed the premises and escaped in a vehicle that had been parked in the lane. An astute onlooker was able to describe the "getaway van" and even gave us a partial licence plate.

"I have heard of a crook's transportation referred to as a 'getaway car' or even a 'getaway vehicle,' but never a 'getaway van,'" I told her.

She looked at me oddly before she said, "It's a three-quarter-ton Dodge, camperized at the factory. It's called a Getaway Van."

I said, "Let me guess . . . you work at a dealership."
She did.

With her excellent description we were able to track the stolen van to a garage on North Road in Coquitlam, and a suspect print was taken from a plastic light cover inside the cab. The robber had taken down the cover in order to pull out the bulb so the light wouldn't illuminate him every time he opened the door while he was on his crime spree throughout the Lower Mainland. Two arrests were made and a witness from the restaurant positively identified the gunman because he had unique eyes, although he never took his helmet off in the course of the robbery. The second suspect had no personal contact with the victims, but he had taken the light cover off, and he was also convicted of armed robbery. That second guilty verdict even surprised me.

Flamingo-cide

My experiences in Stanley Park were not limited to writing tickets and crushing motorcycles. One of the most notorious cases I worked on involved the slaughter of a flock of pink flamingos there. On January 30, 1992, someone broke into the aviary and committed the completely senseless act of maiming and killing all of the resident flamingos. I was assigned the case and attended the park to take in the bloody mess.

This case was a media nightmare. As a similar incident had taken place at a zoo in Hong Kong, the case had international interest as well. There were constant requests for information, and tips kept coming in from armchair experts everywhere. Even a psychic phoned in and offered her services. When I refused to schedule an interview, she began her "reading" over the phone. She said that she "sensed rage, uncontrollable rage." It was probably mine.

Three weeks later, after the tips had dried up, I recommended putting up a reward for information. This strategy was really controversial because the process of setting up a reward was normally reserved for major-crime files, and this was for the most part a case of cruelty to animals. But the reward was posted, information quickly surfaced, and I arrested Jadon Laverge in Maple Ridge soon afterwards. Waiting for Laverge in the Vancouver Police cells was a friend of mine, Constable Brent Alexander, a martial arts instructor and a great policeman, who had been working undercover on another file and was sporting an Aretha Franklin Afro. Alexander's story to Laverge was that, though he—Alexander—was a righteous criminal, he was in jail this time because he had an argument with his girlfriend and she had him arrested after he smashed up their apartment, breaking a birdcage and injuring her bird (whom Alexander had always hated).

Alexander added, "Pit bulls are pets . . . not worthless birds!"

Wanting to impress his new friend, Laverge agreed and proceeded to offer up the details on why he had killed the flamingos at the zoo. He said he needed to show his idiot friends how ruthless he was. Laverge pled guilty to killing the birds as well as breaking and entering and mischief and was sentenced to eight months in prison. On May 13 he escaped from minimum security Ferndale Institution and fled in a waiting car. Two weeks later he was involved in a car chase with the RCMP near Banff, ultimately ditching the car and

Crime Stoppers threw a party to celebrate the arrest of the infamous "Flamingo Killer."

fleeing into the woods. (I can't imagine where he thought he was running to.) Arrested a short time later, he was charged with possession of stolen property.

At the same time that this investigation was going on, the Homicide Unit was dealing with the murder of a young female in the Downtown Eastside. On January 20, 1992, just before 1 a.m., a Canadian Pacific Railway policeman (who happened to be a friend I'd met while playing on the CP Police baseball team) had stealthily approached a van parked suspiciously near Salsbury Drive and Powell Street. As the vehicle sped away, the constable made a note of the licence number. When a dismembered body was located beside a loading bay close to that same spot, police attended a Broadway address to arrest the owner of the van, Bruce Allister, who was later charged with first-degree murder. As sensational as this crime was, members of the Major Crime Squad were quick to note that the killing of a flock of birds in the park was holding a lot more media interest than the murder of a young girl in the Downtown Eastside.

Informants
In the United States, criminals who are caught trafficking in drugs routinely trade up or sell out their suppliers and then go on to inform for their police handlers over the long term, fearing loss of police protection. In the case of serious crime or homicide, the US justice system has a formidable weapon lurking just outside the interview room door: it is called the "three-strike rule." Commit three serious crimes and the punishment is life imprisonment, so whenever the crime involves more than one perpetrator, the first to sprint to the confessional door gets a pass or a reduced sentence as a reward for cooperation.

In Vancouver's criminal environment the concept of cultivating informants and then using them in long-term relationships is far-fetched, because in this country, particularly on the West Coast, the punishment for trafficking is virtually nothing, as is the punishment for most serious crime. And since there is also no threat of serving additional time for failing to cooperate with the police, cultivating police informants is much more of a challenge. However, the police here do tend to have a great number of spontaneous informants. As these are usually drug users who will say or do anything to stay on the street to feed their addiction, the value of their information is limited. I once met an RCMP undercover officer from a medium-sized prairie town whose claim to fame was that he had twenty-three "carded" or formally registered informants. It was not likely true, but it was an assertion that I, or anyone else, could not disprove. I have found that the best information comes from disgruntled wives and girlfriends, ex-wives and ex-girlfriends. (I think you get the picture.)

One of my favourite investigations involved the arrest of one of western Canada's most prolific and successful bank robbers. Jules Thurber was a tall, young, easygoing outdoorsman and about the last person you would have suspected of bank robbery. He spent his time grizzly hunting in the Peace River Country, steelhead fishing in the Skeena and elk hunting in the foothills of the Rocky Mountains. Off-season he would head to Mexico to fish for blue marlin or sailfish. However, the rest of the year he would fund his recreational pursuits by robbing banks in Canada's three western provinces as well as in Washington, Idaho and Montana.

As sometimes happens, a nasty marital dispute resulted in Mrs. Thurber dropping a dime on her wayward spouse by offering up, "You won't believe what my husband does for a living." Once we had Thurber under arrest for multiple robberies, I lined up a friend of mine who was now working undercover to await his arrival at the Vancouver jail. Kenny, my undercover friend, had hair down past his shoulders, a ZZ Top beard and a silver earring in the shape of a dancing skeleton that jangled as he walked. When lodged in the cell that adjoined to where Kenny was waiting, Thurber immediately curled up into the fetal position and repeated, "That bitch . . . that bitch . . . that bitch . . ." I attended Thurber's cell and formally read the eighteen charges of bank robbery I had sworn against him. In shock, he went back to his fetal position on the bunk. When I left the cell, Kenny commented, "Wow! Did you really rob all those banks?" Thurber answered, "Yeah, those and a whole lot more." It was one of the most straightforward confessions I had ever heard.

In the course of conducting hundreds of interviews, I found that about half the time a suspect will offer up a statement of value to the investigation—and not just a matter of saying, "I did it." Even the most hardcore criminal will sometimes lock himself into an alibi that can later be disproved, aiding in prosecution. I found that the most effective way of getting a statement from a criminal was to advise him that I was already aware of all of the facts, and that at this point in the investigation I just wanted to give him an opportunity to tell his side of the story. It's a very effective way of soliciting a confession, because everybody wants to tell his side of the story.

I investigated more than 120 cases between January 1991 and January 1992, the vast majority of which resulted in charges being laid. Then my staff sergeant and I were both transferred to the Robbery Squad, which was another part of the Major Crime Squad, and soon we had a new sergeant, my old classmate Dan Dureau. I worked on that unit for a year with a new partner, investigating a fairly wide range of crimes, from commercial robberies to attempted murders. Whenever a victim was near death, two teams would be assigned, one from Homicide and one from Robbery. If the victim survived, the Robbery Squad would take the file.

A Pet Peeve

I have a lot of pet peeves, but one that really rankles concerns detectives who spend their shifts in the office pretending they are accomplishing something. My personal view is that the only time a detective should be in the office is when he is phoning witnesses to set up interviews or writing up Crown Counsel Reports. Unfortunately, car shortages sometimes give cops the excuse they need to hang out in the office, gossiping, drinking coffee and generally getting into trouble.

Once I was doing a walkabout with our chief constable (my father-in-law) when we passed one of the major-crime offices. An investigator had just photocopied the morning's crossword puzzle (yes, policemen are cheap bastards, almost as cheap as firemen) and was distributing them throughout the office, where his co-workers were huddled around their coffees.

I asked the chief constable, "How can you stand it?"

"We've actually come a long way," he said. "In the old days they would be smoking cigars, drinking Scotch out of those mugs and playing poker at their desks."

One shift when there were no cars available from the motor pool, I asked the staff sergeant if he would speak to the inspector to see if he would loan me his personally assigned car so I could get out on the road and do some work. (Old-school chain of command dictates that a detective doesn't actually speak in person to a commissioned officer.) Even though the inspector usually stayed in his office all day long and rarely left the building, nobody had ever asked to use his car before. Knowing I wouldn't have made the request unless it was important, the staff sergeant passed the inquiry on to the inspector, and then he left the corner office, dangling the keys at me.

Please don't say it, I thought. Don't tell me not to put a scratch on it.

But he said, "The inspector would like to have it back before four."

"No problem," I answered.

I drove around conducting the follow-ups I had to do that day, and then on the way back to the station I noticed that the gas tank was under half full. I pulled into the city-owned Cambie Yards, which was on my route back, and filled up the tank. An idiosyncrasy of the relationship the city budgeting office has with the police department is that it charges the department for a car wash each time the car is filled with gas at the city yards, regardless of whether or not the car is actually washed. As the car wash was about six metres from the gas pumps and it takes about four or five minutes to run the car through it, I usually make an effort to make sure the police department gets what it pays for, and I had the car washed. I came back to the office before four and handed the keys to the staff sergeant. The next morning, we were sitting in the office when the inspector, with a newspaper tucked under his arm, approached his office door. He hesitated there, then detoured back to the staff sergeant's desk, asking loudly enough that the whole office could hear,

"Who borrowed my car yesterday?" The staff sergeant answered (thinking, I suppose, which telephone pole did Cope wrap this one around?), "It was Detective Cope."

By this time the whole office had perked up, ready to witness my notification of transfer. The inspector glanced around the office, having no idea who Detective Cope was, and said, "Well, tell Detective Cope that in future he can borrow my car any time he likes."

In 1992 I competed in the Sergeant's Promotional process again and had a dismal placement in the field of candidates at the Promotional Round Table. Sixteen corporals were to be promoted, and Frank Nordel, the drunken little malingerer from the Traffic Division who scored more than twenty points higher than I did at the Round Table, was going to be one of them. Well, the morning I got the results, I snapped. I wrote a report detailing how the weighting of the numbers used to calculate fitness for promotion was skewed insanely to favour the results of voting by a body of supervisors who were accountable to no one and who had an interest in elevating their own candidates' scores at the expense of more qualified candidates.

My career to that point had been spent out of the public eye, off site at the police academy, Strike Force and the Dog Squad, and I had never joined the clubs that offered high visibility. The result was that after sixteen years of service I was relatively unknown. My report showed that a candidate could score 97 percent on his Fitness for Promotion Report, score maximum points for post-secondary courses taken, attain the highest interview score, have maximum credits for not having taken a sick day in the previous five years, yet he could never be promoted because he had received a low score at the Promotional Round Table.

My report was well written, and I showed it to Sergeant Dureau for his opinion. His response was "Great report. Don't do it." The report was in the departmental mail in the morning, and that afternoon I received a call from the deputy chief's administrative assistant. "Do you have time this afternoon to see the deputy for an interview?"

"Hmm. That was fast," I said to myself. Minutes later I was sitting in front of the deputy chief, who read through my report. "But Wayne," he said, "these are all hypotheticals. You've shown all of these numbers and scores, all of them so high, and yet the Round Table scores so low. These are not based on reality. I can see that you have a problem with the idea of the Round Table, but in real life the weighting you describe could never happen."

"It did happen," I said. "It just happened. Those are my numbers I have used in the report."

"That can't be possible," he said.

"It is possible," I reiterated. "It just happened," and I handed over the hard copy of the scores I had achieved.

He asked what could be done to correct the process, and I told him that the system was so flawed and without credibility that there was no way to fix it. The only possible way to retain it would be to record the proceedings and allow members to grieve any inaccuracies. Even in that case, the process was still doomed because the officers involved would simply have a meeting before the meeting to preordain the outcome. Having nothing to lose, I was steamed but polite. He was a gentleman and seemed to have a genuine interest in fixing the broken model.

An edict was soon published: for the 1993 Promotional Competition, the Round Table component would be scrapped. So Nordel had finally accomplished something of value in his career, having become a catalyst for change to a fair and transparent promotional process.

In the fall of 1992 there would be a shakeup in the Homicide Unit. The management team had decided to toss out the old guard and bring in some new blood. Three senior members were told to pack up their desks. I would be replacing Harold McNaughton, who was away on holiday. Two of the senior members left unceremoniously, with new detectives taking over their desks. My staff sergeant asked me why I hadn't moved my files. I told him I couldn't do that because McNaughton had all of his personal material, photos and case material on his desk. I wasn't going to box up his property while he was away. I would continue working from my Robbery desk, which was about ten metres from the Homicide Unit.

McNaughton returned to work and was surprised to find that he had been transferred. He came over to my desk and took a seat beside me. He said, "Wayne, I know that you had nothing to do with this, and I want to thank you for not moving my stuff. This transfer is completely arbitrary and bullshit. They say they want to get rid of the dead wood, but I have never had a negative comment about my work. I've never had a disciplinary interview, no letters of expectation, never one negative comment. Ever. And regardless of what this management team thinks, I'm not going anywhere. I'm going upstairs to talk to the superintendent right now and straighten this out." So McNaughton went upstairs to speak to the superintendent in charge of the Investigation Division and then remained in Homicide until his retirement.

Imminent transfers weren't expected.

In 1993 I was elected president of the Vancouver Police Detective Association. The majority of voting members were Homicide Squad detectives. There were thirty-four candidates in the

In 1993 I was elected president of the Vancouver Police Detective Association.

1993 Sergeant's Promotional Competition, though it was anticipated there would be only one or two—perhaps three— promotions. The following is a summary of my speech to the Promotional Panel:

> In your average detective squad or police team consisting of ten officers, two of them don't actually accomplish anything. One, the idiot, has already been accounted for. The second officer is for any number of reasons unable to take an investigation to its logical conclusion, which is the conviction of a suspect. Conventional wisdom would be to put the underperformers with more highly motivated officers in an effort to improve productivity. My preference is to put the two together, so when there is a problem, I would usually know where to look. My reasoning is that at least when they are together, they won't be poisoning the efforts of a more dynamic officer.
>
> Four of the officers on the squad will be competent and do the job as required. To these solid professionals, I would offer support, assistance and every level of motivation in an effort to move them to a higher level of productivity. Two or three are senior dedicated officers who will do far more than is expected or required.

To these Type A personalities, I would pretty much offer support and maintain control but stay out of their way.

The remaining one or two are "type double A" and are churning through quality investigations, arrests and convictions on the way to Strike Force, Homicide and Robbery or promotion. These one or two are "rainmakers" and are usually accountable for 70 percent or more of the measurable work done by the squad. My observation has been that the rainmakers require close scrutiny and supervision because their extraordinary performance comes at a cost. They sometimes allow hubris to take them very close to the edge of acceptable practice and sometimes beyond.

Quizzed by the chair of the Promotional Panel about how specifically I would deal with the two officers on the unit who don't actually accomplish anything, I described the usual procedure of monitoring, counselling, letters of expectation and corrective discipline. I summarized by saying that, if these procedures didn't work out, I would give them every dirty, rotten, filthy job that came along, and if they asked why, I would tell them, and anybody else who cared to know, that I was doing it to set an example.

The Chair looked at the other two panel members and said, "Finally . . . finally somebody comes right out and says it."

This time, with the Round Table gone, there was a tie for first place in the Sergeant's Promotional Competition. The person I tied with was an academy classmate of mine, and since we had been sworn in together, our seniority by date was the same. But alphabetically I was first. Her maiden name had started with B, which would have meant she would be the winner by alphabetic seniority, but just prior to joining the force, she had married and now had a surname that started with H. It was a clear win for "Team Cope." In fact, there were five promotions to the rank of sergeant that year; the first three of us were promoted on the same date.

At my Major Crime Squad going-away bash, I got commemorative plaques from both the Robbery Squad and the Homicide Unit. Making the presentation from the Homicide Unit was Harold McNaughton.

Sergeant Cope, 1993–2000

A prisoner being booked at the city jail by a constable: "I think I just shit myself."

"Why don't you tuck your pant leg into your sock?"

"Very funny."

"No, really."

"Okay."

Do Not Pass Go

With my promotion to sergeant came a transfer to the city jail.

Just as some eastern religions have mantras, I have three. One: don't run over the lawnmower cord. Two: don't forget her birthday. Three: don't let anyone die on your jail shift. Failing to chant these mantras appropriately will result in serious consequences, a jail death being the second most dire of the three. I had at least two close calls, both involving addicts. For all of their criminal bravado, I have found that drug addicts are fragile creatures, owing to the fact that they don't take care of themselves physically and they have no idea about the quality and quantity of the poison they inject into their bodies.

The city jail itself is configured so that the sergeant's office has a common wall with the holding cells where everybody who is arrested is held awaiting process. The arrests range from bylaw infractions to the most serious criminal offences.

On one occasion I was working an afternoon shift when we heard a prisoner coming up, screaming and banging against the walls of the elevator. As soon as this idiot was lodged in the cell, he began screaming and kicking at the door, surprising the six or seven more rational cohabitants of the cell with his bizarre antics. Nothing said to him made any difference; he just continued with his disruptive behaviour. The screamer was then moved to the "telephone booth," a cell about two and a half metres by a metre, designed to isolate combative prisoners.

Once he was in this cell, his scream volume increased and he was able to launch himself from the back wall to kick at the door with even more vigour. So we opened the door and applied flex cuffs to his hands and feet, but he continued kicking and screaming at the door from a seated position. I decided to transfer him to the padded cell beside the nurse's station on the fourth floor. I escorted him off the elevator, and, in the company of the two staff nurses, I leaned him up against the wall of the padded cell and returned to my office. A few minutes later I got a call from a nurse; the inmate was still screaming, had torn part of the padding from the door and was kicking at it, disrupting all of the female inmates on that floor. I returned to the padded cell with one of the nurses at my side, rolled the party over on his stomach and used a flex cuff to connect his already tied wrists and ankles together, hog-tying him. I slid the prisoner to the centre of the cell and walked out. As I walked down the hall, the nurse came out of the cell and yelled after me. In the blink of an eye the prisoner had gone from being a screaming, frantic Tasmanian devil to a still and silent corpse. The second staff nurse came out of the office and applied oxygen with the tank. I cut off the flex cuffs that had hog-tied him and he gasped back to life. After he had been treated, I slid him back across the floor and leaned him against the padded wall, where he remained, very, very quietly, for the remainder of the shift.

At that time the concept of positional asphyxiation was unknown, and hog-tying was a legitimate restraint technique for combative and unruly prisoners. This particular prisoner was in his late twenties, reasonably fit and seemingly healthy, and there was no reason to believe that harm would come to him by binding him in this way. Needless to say, I never again restrained a person in this manner.

Killing Time at Work

In late 1993 I got a new compound bow. Hunting season was approaching and I was not going to have an opportunity to sight it in at home. Given that my signature move is to bring my personal weapons from home to work, where I can play with them, I brought the bow to the jail with me. The hallway leading to the jail kitchen was about twenty yards long, a perfect shooting lane. My target was a freestanding archery bullseye made of a dense Styrofoam. When my crew watched me taking the equipment into the elevator upstairs to a vacant floor, I sensed the collective, "Oh no, what is he up to now?" Well, what could go wrong? I set up the target at the far end of the hallway and walked back toward the jail kitchen about fifteen metres. I put on a leather armguard, made a couple of practice draws and then nocked an aluminum arrow.

I sighted and fired. The arrow, travelling at about seventy-five metres per second, launched forward, grazed the right concrete wall and hugged it tight until it hit the far wall. Smashing into the green-tiled brick fifteen metres away, it bent into the shape of a horseshoe and ricocheted back, spinning like one of the villain's razored chariot wheels in Ben-Hur, somehow missing me as it went past at chest level. It clattered to a stop in the kitchen, which was still unoccupied at the time.

I packed up all of the gear and headed back to my office. "That didn't take long," the booking officer commented.

"No, it's all tuned up," I answered.

Jailhouse *Jeopardy!* vs. Clarence Darrow

Visiting hours at the jail are from eight to eleven in the morning, then from five to seven in the evening. Usually there are very few visitors because the Vancouver jail is not a long-term or even medium-term holding facility, although there were cases when prisoners had to be held over a few days or a weekend. Our goal, therefore, was to have the scrotes tucked peacefully away in their cells by 7:25 p.m., because 7:30 was the time for Jailhouse *Jeopardy!*

In Jailhouse *Jeopardy!* the rules were slightly different than regular *Jeopardy!* All of the members of the team would gather around the booking desk television and get ready to shout out the questions to the answers. The first difference was that answers didn't have to be given in the form of a question, and the second was that you weren't penalized for wrong answers. It was extremely helpful if you were a quick study and could finish reading the answer on the screen before anybody else. It was kind of like being a fighter pilot in the First World War—the flyer with the best eyesight and fastest trigger finger generally won the battle.

Answering the phone in the jail was discouraged between 7:30 and 8 p.m., but one Friday night about ten minutes before eight, the phone rang when we were in the middle of "Double Jeopardy," and one of the guards answered the phone.

Guard: "Sergeant Cope, it's for you."

Me: "I'm not in."

Guard: "It's a lawyer."

Me: "Oh, all right. Hello, Sergeant Cope speaking."

Clarence Darrow: "I would like to come in this evening to speak to my client."

Me: "I'm sorry. That's not going to be possible. Visiting hours are between five and seven."

Clarence: "I'm not a visitor. I'm his lawyer."

Me: "The hours are the same. We are far too busy up here to orchestrate personal, individual visits."

Clarence: "I'm not a visitor. I'm his lawyer."

Me: "If you would like to come by tomorrow, visiting hours are between eight and eleven, then five to seven."

Clarence: "I'm coming down there right now, and I am going to pound on that elevator until you let me in."

Me: "I wouldn't advise that."

(Cue the "Final Jeopardy" music playing loudly in the background)

Clarence: "Are you watching *Jeopardy!*?"

Me: "No."

Clarence: "You're watching *Jeopardy!*, aren't you? I'm coming down there right now, and I'm going to pound on that door until you let me in to see my client."

Me: "I wouldn't advise that. We have a lot of prisoners here now who need their rest. If you come down and pound on the doors, I'll have you arrested for disturbing the peace, and I'll make sure you are lodged on a different floor than your client."

Clarence: "That's it! I'm reporting you to the duty officer. I'm going to phone him right now and tell him you're watching *Jeopardy!*. What's the duty officer's phone number?"

Me: "I don't have that information, as I rarely call him. I could give you the number for Internal Affairs, but they won't be open until eight on Monday morning. Maybe you can drop in to see them on your way to visit your client."

Clarence: (Silence.)

Click.

Get Me Out of Here

About nine months into my tour of duty at the jail, I spoke to my staff sergeant, Gerry Baker, and asked about the timeline relating to my transfer. I wanted to remind him that working at the jail had not been my career choice and that when it came to planning my exit, sooner would be better than later. He asked if I had any preferences regarding transfer, and I told him that I was easy to please. Any patrol sergeant's position was fine, but since I had spent my previous patrol duty in the northwest sector, if possible I would like to try something new.

The next time I met up with Baker, he said, "Your transfer is set for the end of the month. You will be going to Team 2."

Team 2, of course, is in the heart of the northwest sector. I said, "Gerry, do you remember the part of our conversation where I said I wanted to go anywhere but Patrol Northwest?"

It was as though a light went on. "That's right," he said. "You said you didn't want to go there. I'll go back and get that changed, though I can't promise your transfer will be made this shift change."

"Okay, don't worry about it," I said. "It doesn't really matter." While I would have preferred to work in an area of the city I had never worked before, a high volume of arrests were made in Patrol Northwest, and I knew that I would be kept busy. As it turned out, I was assigned to supervise a great new crew of people back at Vancouver's epicentre—the Granville Mall.

The Suicide Locker

In 1994 we were relocated to a new building at the south foot of the Cambie Street Bridge. Furnishing the premises had been going on for over a year, and the new facilities included ergonomic workstations, fitness facilities, even purpose-built lockers with ample room for personal uniform storage. Being allowed to select your new locker was a game changer. Because of the nature of the workforce, police officers would normally wait out the transfer or retirement of other members and move their personal property in as property was moved out. But if you knew of an impending transfer, you would approach the exiting officer, perhaps with a gratuity, in exchange for his keys. When you're working in a sea of insanity, little creature comforts like having a good locker are very important to police officers. A locker's desirability was contingent on close proximity to the toilet (bad), distance to the common hall and the elevator (good), whether it was a corner unit (good), proximity to idiots (bad) as well as the general condition and age of the unit (good or bad). As well as the key issued by the police stores keeper, officers would secure their lockers with their own padlocks.

My squad was pretty much one of the first to transfer to the new building, so I attended stores and was told to go to the new building, locate a locker that was free (unlocked) and return with the number of the locker in order to get the key. I couldn't believe what I was hearing. This assignment plan was fundamentally flawed because until all of the lockers were assigned, the stores officer would have no way of controlling allocation. I hurried down to the Army and Navy Department Store, picked up two good locks and headed over to the new building. In the changing room, virtually all of the lockers were empty. I picked the choicest corner unit closest to the door and the elevator and farthest from the toilet. I put one of my locks on this locker and one on the locker beside it, safe in knowing that there was no roster being kept of empty lockers, just the ones that were occupied.

Once the giddiness of dual locker ownership began to wear off, I thought, what am I going to do with this locker that I want but don't need? Then, in a flash, it came to me: it will become a locker for my pristine dress uniform with its shiny medals and polished chrome buttons and buckles and my spit-polished shoes. (Actually, you don't have to polish the chrome accoutrement, as they stay pretty shiny when left alone.) But something was missing. I had a rightly earned reputation for being eccentric, so I bought an expensive bottle of Scotch (I don't drink Scotch but it completed the effect) and put it on the upper shelf beside my hat. I brought in my Smith & Wesson stainless steel .357 Magnum from home and laid it beside the Scotch, then stood a single round of ammunition upright beside it. And the legend of Cope's Suicide Locker was born. From time to time I got requests from friends to see it. Several years and a few transfers later, I got a brusque message from Internal Affairs: "We opened your lockers. You can pick up your uniforms from stores. Your gun is at the range." I don't recall getting the Scotch back.

Me, speaking in defence of two constables who had their picture taken with an "exotic dancer" in support of a local charity drive: "She wasn't naked. She was wearing cowboy boots."

Meanwhile Out on Patrol

One fall evening as I was driving down the Granville Mall, there was a call about a man with a knife who was threatening people three blocks away. I attended the east side of the 1100 block in time to see three or four police officers circling a deranged male who—surprisingly—was on the pay phone to 9-1-1. As he screamed threats and obscenities (all recorded on the phone) to the crowd, a member of the Emergency Response Team pulled up beside me and popped open his trunk. As the officer loaded a cannon with some kind of projectile, I asked, "What is that?"

He answered, "It's an ARWEN [Anti-Riot Weapon Enfield] gun."

I asked, "Is it non-lethal?"

"With this ammunition it is," he said, displaying a bean-bag-type round.

I looked over at the crazy man dodging around with his knife extended, threatening everybody in the vicinity, and said, "Shoot him."

The constable said, "What was that?"

I reiterated, "Shoot him. Right now."

Kaboom.

The acting duty officer rolled up on the curb just in time to hear the cannon blast, looked over at me and asked, "What did we do now?"

I answered, "I just approved the deployment of the ARWEN, and a suspect who had been threatening the public with a knife has been taken into custody."

"You authorized deployment, did you?" the acting duty officer asked.

"Yes, sir, I did."

And without another word he looked forward and drove northbound down the Mall.

One fortunate turn occurred during my time on the Granville Street beat. While attending the Nelson Place Hotel, we visited its club, the BaBalu, where a teenaged phenom was singing several times a week. This youngster wore a fedora and did an incredible job crooning out songs from the Sinatra era. For a while we actually planned our attendance to the area based on when Michael Bublé would be singing. Of course, he wasn't there long.

Management

I had a really good relationship with our management team. Our staff sergeant, Dave Mackie-Dean, told me about his first meeting with our new inspector.

Inspector: "There are only two things you have to understand about how this office is run. Number one is my desk, and number two is 2:45."

Mackie-Dean: "What about the desk?"

Inspector: "See how meticulously clean it is? Not one pen out of place, not one pencil, not one scrap of paper on it."

Mackie-Dean: "Yes, I see that, sir."

Inspector: "That's because every single letter, report, paper, memo or file that comes to my desk is immediately placed on your desk, where you will deal with it. Think of it as an administrative evaluation for your next promotion. If anything ever comes back to me, I'll be grading you on whether or not it had been completed up to 'our standards.'"

Mackie-Dean: "Understood, sir. And 2:45—what is the significance of that?"

Inspector: "That is my tee-off time. Every day."

The Scavenger Hunt

West Vancouver is a small municipality located a short trip across Burrard Inlet by way of the Lions Gate Bridge. It boasts some of the toniest neighbourhoods in Vancouver's Lower Mainland with the highest average income in Canada, though there is an ongoing cultural clash in this municipality between the arrogant rich who think that petty bylaws don't apply to them and an overzealous bylaw enforcement cadre who don't like self-absorbed rich scofflaws. I have booked in West Vancouver citizens who had warrants outstanding for fishing off the wrong side of the Capilano Bridge as well as ignoring stop-work orders relating to home renovations.

While West Van boasts one of Canada's most affluent postal codes, just across the Inlet is the Downtown Eastside, which boasts one of the poorest. Nevertheless, pupils of one of the most prestigious private schools in West Vancouver thought that it would be a good idea to have a scavenger hunt involving the Downtown Eastside. On the list of items that had to be checked off was the acquisition of a billiard ball from one of the skid row bars. When a carload of preppies descended on one of our seediest establishments and attempted to liberate a few of the balls, the local drug crowd laid a beating on the trust fund kids and tossed them into the street. The five kids regrouped and came up with a master plan. One of the group was elected to run into the bar, grab a ball off of the pool table and make a dash for the car parked just outside the door. The hero burst through the entrance, ran for a table and made a grab for the ball. A throng of patrons descended on him, one of them pulling out a knife. The next scene had the disoriented youth staggering back out of the bar toward his compatriots on the street, trying to stuff his intestines back into his shirt. That was what we saw when we arrived at the same time as the ambulance and another carful of dimwits from the private school. As the victim was being attended to and loaded into the ambulance, I was approached by one of the new arrivals, who nodded acknowledgment toward his wounded friend. Then he pulled out his list and asked, "Officer, can you tell me exactly which way it is to the Nine O'Clock Gun?"

Strike Force—Round Two

Because there were too many sergeants vying for too few jobs in Strike Force, transferring back there took about two years longer than I wanted it to, but in 1997 I was back. The dynamic of the unit had been completely changed by the elimination of the corporal/detective rank two years earlier. The term "detective" was now a job description, not a rank, and in real terms this meant that constables were doing all Strike Force jobs, including supervision and training.

On my first tour of duty with the unit, the sergeant had two detectives coordinating the investigations, surveillance, training and supervision. Now there was just one sergeant on each squad, dealing with nine Type A personalities. As a result, the unit has been a revolving door for sergeants. I had a one-on-one with a sergeant who was leaving who confided, "Wayne, I don't know what they are doing out there. I don't understand the way they do surveillance. I just stay in the office and do the paperwork while they are out there chasing crooks."

My first contact with one of the detective constables was when I sat through the STAR (Surveillance Tactics and Resources) course I had co-written in 1986. On the first day of training, the constable in charge asked smugly, "Have any of you even read the manual prior to coming here today?" I suppose I got off on the wrong foot when I told him that I had actually written the manual. I couldn't help but notice that my name and the names of my two co-authors had been struck from the front page.

But regardless of the issues relating to command, I had an extremely effective crew. They had an outstanding "road boss," the constable in charge of day-to-day surveillance, but I had all members rotate through that position in an effort to train new people for the job. Previously there had been such a failure of supervision on the unit that the squad had come to believe that the "road boss" was also in charge of the investigations. On several occasions I had to re-direct the team that the instructions given by the road boss could be countermanded at any time by the sergeant. Incredibly, that train of thought met with general resistance from the unit.

One of My Biggest Regrets

I enjoyed Strike Force work because it was highly technical when it came to mobile surveillance, and the files usually terminated with a dramatic arrest immediately following the crime. Our preferred surveillance was on bank robbers, who, at that time, were near the top of the criminal food chain. On one occasion we had been conducting surveillance for about ten days on a crew that had been planning a bank robbery in the southwest sector of the city. Criminals who are about to commit a major crime do a lot of counter-surveillance initially, but then once they convince themselves that they are in the clear, their behaviour becomes completely relaxed. We had been following this three-man crew (actually two men and one woman) as they cruised the southwest part of the city, and they had just gone into a very calm mode, meaning that the robbery was imminent. As we followed them, I noticed Jack Webster, a TV talk-show host and one of Vancouver's finest reporters, standing at the corner of 41st Avenue and Granville Street, waiting for someone. I was absolutely torn. I wanted so badly to pull up beside him, identify myself and say, "Jack, would you like to watch a bank robbery in progress and then watch us arrest the crew? Hop in." But I couldn't do it. The crew did their robbery at 49th and Granville; we conducted surveillance as they sped away from the scene and arrested them as they left the area.

Me: "Your honour, this is trickery. Defence counsel is engaging in trickery."

Federal Court Judge (looking up from his crossword puzzle): "What's that?"

Me: "I say that defence counsel is engaging in trickery. He is substituting metric for standard, altering the measurements to confuse."

Judge (frowning at the defence table): "What do you have to say about that?"

Counsel: "I just thought I would throw a few numbers out there."

Judge: "Keep it up and I'll be throwing out your defence."

Counsel: "No more questions, m'Lord."

The Drug Squad

In 1997 the Investigation Division suffered a severe shortage of investigators, and a decision was made to vapourize one of the three Strike Force units and distribute the detective constables throughout the division. At the same time I was advised that my services would be welcomed on the VPD Drug Squad. I didn't have a problem with the move because there were some highly motivated officers working in the Drug Squad. We had a real mix of personnel, three of whom were senior to me, which made them real old-timers.

At that time we were just in transition into computers, and everybody was being issued a desktop computer terminal. I really never thought that I would see the day when old-school policemen would be sitting at a desk, typing away on their files, and I thought that Nelson Schooner, our most senior police detective, might have some issues with all of the new changes. It turned out he was probably the fastest typist on the squad and in spite of some minor setbacks had no problem learning electronic records processing. But one day he advised me that his computer had stopped working. He unplugged it, restarted it, rebooted it, control-alt-deleted it, all to no avail. Nothing, no power at the cord, no activity on the screen, and he wanted to call tech support. But his desk was directly across from mine, and I looked over and told him, "Nelson, your monitor is off."

"I know," He responded. "The whole thing's not working. It's buggered."

"Nelson, it's just like your TV set at home, I said," Your VCR is turned on, your receiver is turned on, but now you have to turn on the TV. The button is down there."

"The TV has its own button?"

"Yes, Nelson, the TV has its own button."

On another occasion he got upset with me because I unplugged his phone, which would ring continuously while he was out of the office. He said, "How am I supposed to get my messages if you unplug it?"

"Nelson, there is no little man in that phone taking messages for you," I said. "The calls come into an answering system that works regardless of whether or not your phone is actually plugged in."

"Are you sure?" he asked.

"Yes, Nelson, I'm sure."

Having recently arrived from Strike Force, I was fairly meticulous about surveillance technique. One day we were taking a break from our usual grow op warrant executions and were going to spend the evening following some organized-crime types. I decided on the car assignments and wrote them up on the office whiteboard, designating who would be conducting mobile surveillance (driving) and who would "wire up" and be the passenger in case the target went out on foot. Robert Bell was a young, hard-working detective constable who sat immediately behind me in the office. He looked up at the board to see that he was assigned to work with Nelson and said, "I'm not riding in the same car as him. He drives like an idiot." I was surprised by the very public discord and turned to face him. "If you have a legitimate reason for not wanting to work with Detective Schooner, we can talk about it privately."

There are lots of reasons why two police officers shouldn't be in the same car together. One could be dating the other's ex-wife, one could be the other's love child, or maybe the two just hate each other. All are legitimate reasons for maintaining a distance.

Bell answered immediately: "There is no other reason. He is too dangerous a driver. I'm not getting in a car with him."

"Well, I have driven with Detective Schooner," I responded. "And I think that he is a particularly good driver." And he was, though like all good surveillance personnel, he drove fast.

"Well, I'm not driving with him," Bell said.

At this point the whole office went quiet. People started edging closer to see what was coming next.

"Robert, I want you to understand in the clearest possible terms that I have set up the surveillance roster for the evening, and that I am directing you to work with Detective Schooner."

"I'm not doing it," Bell said.

Those who had been moving closer for a better vantage point were now edging away so they would not have to give evidence at the upcoming disciplinary inquiry. "Bob," I relented, "we're going to take a break for fifteen minutes, so grab a coffee with the crew. I think they can be found hiding in the hall. I want you to ask for their advice on this matter. In the meantime, I'm going to draft a written order and have it ready for you when you get back."

Bell returned in about ten minutes and told me that he was looking forward to spending the rest of the shift driving with Detective Schooner.

The next time we did mobile surveillance, I left the assignment blocks open on the whiteboard so the crew could fill their names in themselves.

The bulk of our work involved locating the many commercial marijuana grow ops in the city. At any given time the squad had a list of more than 250 commercial grow ops that were awaiting our arrival with warrant and battering ram. The greatest concentration of grow ops we observed was four on one block. In 1999 we shut down 203 operations, and in the vast majority of cases charges were laid. Based on a valuation relating to the termination of one crop per premise, my ten-man squad cost the illegal drug-growing community over forty-six million dollars. Using several methods of calculating the total number of operations in the city, I determined that there were approximately 3,500, each with an average value of $227,000 a crop. Unlike with outdoor farming, each indoor

Some pretty healthy marijuana plants found at one of Vancouver's several thousand illegal commercial grow ops. The number of operations running in Vancouver today is only a small fraction of those that prospered in the late 1990s.

operation could average three crops a year, so in 1999 the value of commercial marijuana operations within the city of Vancouver was $2,383,500,000. More than two billion dollars. The vast majority of the product was exported to the United States, where it was selling for $3,000 a pound in Washington state and $9,000 a pound in southern California.

The reason for the high prices paid for "BC Bud" is that the THC (the psychoactive component) level was more than 12 percent (and sometimes more than 20 percent), compared to the 1 or 2 percent that had been typical in the plants of the 1960s and 1970s. The obvious question is, since these were indoor grow ops, many of them hydroponic and independent of climate, why didn't their American customers just grow their own? The answer is simple. This kind of operation involved a lot of brick and mortar, and at minimum required the farmer to be anchored to the same location for three months per crop, which meant that locating and charging an operator, while time-consuming, was relatively straightforward using fingerprinting and the documents that were found on location. With the severity of punishment handed out on their side of the border, the Americans couldn't afford to get caught.

I could never understand the mentality of the Canadian courts when dealing with drug offences. In Canada there is no credible punishment associated with production and trafficking in marijuana. Time and time again we would present the courts with producers, showing the tax-free profits they were hoping to reap, and time and time again the result would be conviction, a small fine and probation. American drug producers would expect to spend years in prison for an offence that would be dealt with as a trivial malfeasance in Vancouver. Even if West Coast courts believe, as they appear to, that trafficking and use of narcotics should be legalized, one would think that they would be offended by and punish those earning hundreds of thousands of dollars in untaxed income per crop cycle.

I discovered there were three main types of grow ops, the vast majority of which were located in rental housing. Approximately 80 percent of these operations were run by Vietnamese, and they were typified by smaller plants that were grown in a three-month cycle in an attempt to run four crops a year. These grow ops were scrupulously clean and usually had a religious icon above the living room doorway. At times a family would be living on the main floor while a grow op was running in the basement, but in the course of investigating hundreds of these, I never once saw any indication that the farmers were using the product themselves. No ashtrays with stubbed out roaches.

One night my crew and I were having dinner at a Vietnamese restaurant when the owner approached us and complained that she and her husband couldn't get staff to work for them because all the young people in their community were employed in the marijuana growing industry. Shortly after that we crashed through the door of a Vietnamese grow op to find it being guarded by a newly arrived university student, who was studying at a desk stacked high with books. Recognizing that he was the caretaker of the crop rather than the owner and profiteer, we made him an offer he couldn't refuse. Tell us his story, we said, and we would let him go. He told us that he had recently arrived from Vietnam and was immediately approached by growers who attempted to recruit him into their organization. He refused, telling the group that he didn't want to get into trouble with the police or the courts. They advised him that the courts didn't take narcotics charges seriously, and even if he was charged and convicted, nothing would happen to him. To reinforce this, they invited him to attend the federal drug court and see what punishments were being meted out. He sat in for a few trials, observed that in fact there was no credible punishment associated with the offence and advised his newly found friends that he was "in."

The second type of operation was the biker grow op, typified by very large plants and expensive, state-of-the-art equipment. Much less care was taken in these operations to keep the areas clean, weapons were much more likely to be present and they were more likely to show creativity. While Vietnamese grow ops were cookie cutter with little variation, the biker grow ops demonstrated all manner of ingenuity involving irrigation, CO_2 infusion, expulsion of exhaust, and camouflage. One of the telltale clues of a typical basement operation is the covered windows, which allow the farmer to regulate the lighting in order to trick the plants into going through a summer and fall cycle over the course of two months, rather than six, thereby accelerating maturity. One of the biker grow ops had slatted blinds partially obscuring the large basement window. By peering through the slats, you could see a couch, dresser and lamp in the basement bedroom. But all of this had been painted on a large canvas about two feet back from the window to fool any drug-squad snoopers. In another grow op the whole of the downstairs had been clad in lead in an effort to thwart thermal imaging equipment. It didn't.

Whenever we busted one of these grow ops, I always measured the internal and external dimensions of the building to ensure that we didn't miss any hidden areas. In several homes we found secret rooms, sometimes with a hidden caretaker. But most clandestine operations are exposed because of the horrendous stench that marijuana makes in the last few weeks of its growth cycle. A healthy crop requires a massive circulation of air, with a preferred infusion of carbon dioxide from compressed tanks. Growers typically vent the air in the evenings to avoid public scrutiny, so this is when the skunky smell is at its worst. The most effective venting system involves tapping into the sewer line through the house's toilet outflow and thereby expelling the exhaust away from the house.

The third type of operation, which constituted only a small minority of the total, was the hippy grow op. These were independent, not necessarily for-profit endeavours run by individuals with a rebellious streak. Sometimes they were growing it to provide medical marijuana to those in need, and sometimes they were growing it just to prove they could. And many of them were users who preferred to grow their own crops so they didn't have to buy it on the illegal market.

For my first two years on the Drug Squad I found the work very interesting. We would work ten-hour days, usually starting in the afternoon, four days a week. In addition to our regular shifts that sometimes resulted in overtime, we would also be called into court an average of twice a week during our off time and then be called out another couple of evenings a week when the Patrol Division walked into a grow operation and required assistance with the investigation. As a result, there came a time when I was ready for a change.

The Historical Homicide Unit, 2001–06

The officer in charge of the Homicide Unit at a sector meeting, mustering his most condescending and dismissive tone: "Wayne, are you telling me you honestly and truly believe that a serial killer is out there murdering these missing women?"

Me: "I'm not saying I honestly and truly believe it. I am just saying we should consider the possibility."

The Grieving Process

In 1999 I got a call from an old friend who was a sergeant in command of one of the teams at the Provincial Unsolved Homicide Unit, a joint forces operation run by the RCMP. It was made up of four integrated teams with six members on each team; their mandate was to travel the province and review open but cold homicide files. My friend was retiring and thought I should apply for his job.

The administrative protocol was that Vancouver Police Department investigators were first assigned to the Homicide Unit before being seconded to the Provincial Unsolved Homicide Unit. My application for the job was buoyed by the fact that I had previous homicide experience: while with the Robbery Unit, I had investigated three murders, two as an initial investigator on the scene and the third as a primary investigator (the murder of Helene Flanders, a Vancouver cold case).

I got a phone call from Frank Duchesne, a detective in Staff Development, who advised me that I had scored the highest in the competition for both of the sergeant's positions that had become available in the Homicide Unit, and that I would be given the choice of the two jobs, one in current and the other in historical. I opted for the Unsolved Homicide Unit because I thought investigating cold cases would be a lot more interesting than trying to determine who was responsible for the latest gangland hit for which Vancouver was becoming famous. When the inspector in charge of Homicide called to welcome me on board, I asked if he wanted me to coordinate the mechanics of the transfer with Staff Development, or if he wanted to do it. He advised that he would do it. Then a few weeks later I was told that there had been some irregularities in the selection process (a candidate had been asked to pull his application because he had recently completed a tour of duty with the Homicide Unit) and that the competition was to be reopened. I met with the deputy chief constable to express my concerns (he was not the likeable one who had just restructured the promotional system at my request), and he encouraged me to reapply for the position. I advised him that I wouldn't be reapplying for a job I had already been awarded and that I would give him twenty-four hours to change his mind about reopening the competition. Following that, I would be filing a grievance with the union.

"I take that as a threat," he said.

"Don't take it as a threat," I said. "I'm just telling you what I am going to do."

I gave him two days and then walked into the union office to discuss the circumstances with the union president. He read through my report, which, while completely true, detailed many more of the nuances and politics that I felt had led to the reposting of the position. He said, "Wayne, I am going to tell you three things. One, you have the job. That is an absolute given. Two, don't go to the media with this information. And three, if there is a civil action relating to this, let us use our union lawyers."

I agreed, and the battle began. It started with me being interviewed by Internal Affairs, where I noticed that a copy of the report I had prepared relating to the grievance that I had forwarded to the senior management team was numbered with a felt marker. I asked the investigator about the significance of the number and was told that they were just trying to limit access to the information. I told him that as far as I was concerned, every word was true and they could photocopy the report and place it in the mail for each of Vancouver's 1,100 officers to read. At the same time that I was being investigated, my Drug Squad subordinates were questioned regarding possible weaknesses in my leadership and command style. The enquiry went on for about six months. I was in the middle of a departmental scandal. Unlike in the RCMP, where the slightest provocation resulted in a grievance, it was unheard of that a VPD sergeant should be grieving treatment at the hands of the Vancouver force. I would walk into a room and everyone would stop talking. Ultimately I was offered the sergeant's job with Vancouver's Homicide Unit. I refused the compromise. A few days later I was called back to the Homicide inspector's office, where he shook my hand, congratulated me on my perseverance and told me that I was the VPD's new sergeant at the Provincial Unsolved Homicide Unit.

I arrived at the Provincial Unsolved Homicide Unit in March 2001, about six months after I had first been awarded the job. My retired friend was long gone, and the interim sergeant—the same one who had been asked to pull his application from the initial selection process—had participated successfully in the second competition. With my arrival, he was offered an opportunity to take a position with Vancouver's regular Homicide Unit. The transition was smooth and I was pleasantly surprised to find that he had left me a comprehensive written summary of all the work done in the course of the previous year, as well as a prioritized to-do list relating to current investigations.

However, once at the RCMP's Surrey satellite office, I found that my access to Vancouver personnel was severely limited because one of the requirements for selection to the job was that the applicant should have previous homicide investigation experience. On first blush, it seemed like a logical prerequisite except that the Vancouver detectives currently with the Homicide Unit would then decide for themselves which of their members was most deserving of the job and forward only that one application.

There is an air of arrogance and entitlement that exists in some high-profile specialty squads. On several occasions I have seen young, inexperienced constables come begging at the door for an opportunity to join an elite unit (Strike Force, Dog Squad, Major Crime Squad, Homicide or Robbery) and, once on that unit, acquire a hubris offensive to the peasants not assigned to that cadre. They somehow come to believe that they can't be replaced. In reality, everybody leaves eventually, and there is always somebody waiting who can do the job. I have never been intimidated by this bluff and bluster. Probably because I have served on many of the elite squads, I would look at these strutting peacocks and think: I have worked with giants, and you are not one of them. A sobering remedy for this egotism would be to set firm limits on tenure for specialty units and ensure that promotion meant immediate transfer back to patrol or even to my personal favourite, the jail, where the new sergeant can reacquaint himself with the reality of day-to-day policing. When I arrived at the Historical Homicide Unit, I immediately revised the job description to direct that any Major Crime Squad (MCS) investigative experience would be a sufficient prerequisite for the job. My interpretation of MCS investigative experience included Robbery, Sex Crimes and even Strike Force.

Besides acting as a supervisor to five detectives—one of them a detective from the VPD—my job description as a sergeant with Unsolved Homicides was nebulous enough to allow me to review my own files and conduct my own investigations, so I had my business cards revised to show my rank as detective sergeant. The RCMP staff sergeant in charge of the unit once asked me about the rank that accompanied my signature block, saying that he hadn't realized that the VPD had detective sergeants. My answer was: "It has one." As previously described, the corporal/detective and the staff sergeant ranks had been eliminated in the VPD and the sergeant's position was made purely supervisory. Since then, the Professional Standards section (Internal Affairs), formerly manned by corporal/detectives, has been populated by sergeants who conduct investigations, and the rank of staff sergeant has been restored.

The identities of the victims that I describe in this chapter and the circumstances surrounding their deaths are all a matter of public record. However, some murderers, who understandably go to great lengths to avoid capture, once exposed revel in the publicity and notoriety of their crimes. I refuse to give these monsters additional press and in most cases have assigned these killers fictional names.

Unsolved Homicide Unit: Day One

When I arrived, my unit was just wrapping up the investigation of Jimmy James, who had been the subject of a Mr. Big Crime Boss sting. I think most people have a hard time wrapping their minds around the fact that criminals routinely blab to each other about the evils they have committed. In modern times the fastest confession ever obtained by the RCMP Undercover Unit was obtained in the first words out of the mouth of a suspect in an initial meeting between the target and the undercover officer.

A "Mr. Big" sting involves conducting a background investigation of a person suspected of murder and then arranging a meeting with an RCMP undercover member who pretends to be a mid-level criminal working for a crime boss and his criminal empire. The target (suspect) works his way into the organization, committing a series of staged criminal scenarios with his new undercover RCMP pal; these can include counterfeiting, diamond smuggling, arms purchasing, extortion and even murder. If the suspect has a background in firearms, the officer avoids firearms, and if the suspect is a white-collar criminal, the officer avoids white-collar crime, because the idea is to knock the target out of his comfort zone. After three or four months of simulated criminal activity, where the suspect has worked his way up the organization's food chain, he will be given an opportunity to participate in a big score. That is, if Mr.

Big can put forces in play to erase all evidence related to the suspect's inconvenient past crime, details of which have surfaced in the course of the target's association with his new best friend. In order to do this, Mr. Big must hear about every minute detail of the suspect's personal involvement in the crime. Roll the tape.

To achieve status as undercover officers, RCMP members have to take and pass the "undercover course," which culminates in the officer being put on the street in an unfamiliar town, where he must survive on the street without funds, begging, borrowing or conning a set amount of cash to be delivered to the instructors at the end of the day. With graduation the officers are assigned a UC (undercover) number and are authorized to participate in local undercover operations. Very few of these operators work at the job full-time but are called upon to be bit players in larger undercover operations run by the full-time undercover unit. Members qualified to participate in undercover scenarios number in the hundreds, while the full-time British Columbian UC team numbers only about sixteen.

The "bit players" pretend to be gunrunners, diamond smugglers, counterfeiters and even hit men. The full-time members do the closer, one-on-one work with the target in an effort to gain his confidence and ultimately a confession. Every principal operator in an undercover scenario is covered full-time by another operator who is unseen by the suspect and monitors activity (and safety) by surreptitious audio transmission. While the location of the undercover team's office is a closely guarded secret, I noticed that, when meeting with their members, they would always be about five minutes away from one of the larger shopping centres in the Lower Mainland. I used to joke with them that I was going to follow them back to their bat cave, but I thought the joke was funnier than they did.

The Mr. Big Program has a success rate in the low 90 percent range, both in charging and excluding from suspicion those thought to be responsible for a crime. However, generally speaking, the program doesn't work on gang members, the wealthy and the crazy. Gang members already belong to a criminal empire and are not likely to join a new one, and the cash earned by joining a risky new enterprise usually won't tempt rich people. Crazy people are unable to deal with and participate in the logical progression of criminal activity that leads to a confession. The courts have ruled that Mr. Big ruses can involve any activity that doesn't offend community standards. Basically, any crime scenario is allowed that involves the same crime being investigated or a lesser crime than the one the suspect was thought to have committed. So, for officers investigating a murder, the gloves were off and simulation of any crime was allowed.

Jimmy James had been difficult to locate, but Adrian Cockney, one of the Vancouver detectives on my unit, found him just by focusing on skid row, where James had spent most of his life, and visually identifying him as he walked down the street. One would think that in modern times, it would be relatively simple to locate criminals like Jimmy, but if the target is not on welfare, parole or probation and does not surface on the police computer database, it can be a real problem. And this problem is compounded by the fact that the police can't just ask around the neighbourhood, because that would telegraph their interest in the suspect. As it turned out, Jimmy was in such bad financial straits that he would frequent the bars in the area in order to steal rolls of toilet paper from their washrooms.

After initial contact was made with the RCMP under-cover member, Jimmy was given a series of jobs to do and became an enthusiastic participant in his new crime family. Apparently this boost in confidence and self-esteem stirred up his long-dormant homicidal disposition, which was revealed when he arrived at the airport on his way to see Mr. Big with his thumb wrapped in a bandage. He explained that days earlier he had completed another contract hit. Jimmy knocked on the victim's door in North Vancouver and, after a short conversation, shot him in the chest with a small-calibre pistol. When the victim rushed him, Jimmy put up his hand to push his target back into the entryway and fired again, shooting off part of his own thumb. Jimmy then confessed everything to the undercover operators and even took them on a "show and tell" to locate previously secreted weapons. He ultimately confided that over the course of the past twenty years, he had murdered on four occasions.

One particularly interesting element of the case was that, buried in one of the homicide files, there was an evaluation of James as a suspect written by one of the original investigators. The detective had noted that James was a passive, non-violent sort, one simply not capable of committing such a cold-blooded crime. This report has always stood out in my mind because it was just not the type of observation that would normally be included in a report. James was, in fact, such a sociopathic charmer that the investigator had gone out of his way to comment on his likely innocence. I have seen similar inappropriate comments in other reports, and to me they shine like a flare in the night, signalling that the suspect requires closer examination.

Another flag that a suspect requires close scrutiny: he quits drinking alcohol after the homicide. Abstinence signals two things. First, that the suspect had been drinking at the time of the incident and wants to ensure that there is no similar reoccurrence, and second, the suspect recognizes that drunkenness might cause him to make an unfortunate disclosure about the crime. Some members of the undercover team call alcohol the truth serum, so as long as the target remains coherent and on mission, there is every reason to encourage consumption.

Cody and Graham: A Double Homicide in Lillooet, BC

A new file my unit was investigating involved the murder of two victims from Lillooet, BC. These males lived in houses side by side, both of which had been torched after the murders. It was decided that a prize from some fictional entity would precipitate the initial contact with the target. On April 3 I authorized the purchase of seven tickets for a Kelowna Rockets hockey game. Two tickets were for the suspect and his guest, and two were for the co-winner of the prize, a friendly but shady character who seemed to have a lot of money, and his girlfriend, who were, of course, two RCMP undercover members. The contact was made when the limo that came to pick up the target also carried the surprisingly amicable co-winners. The rest of the tickets went to the undercover officers who would physically cover (watch) the interaction between the suspect and the primary undercover contacts.

Over the course of the next month, the target was run from one end of the province to the other, participating in a number of simulated criminal scenarios constructed to make him believe he was moving up in a criminal organization. The suspect was so in awe of the undercover operator that he began to dress like him and even, like his new boss, play

Spanish music on the radio. At dinner on April 23 in Earls restaurant in Kamloops, the target ordered calamari—even though he had no idea what it was—because that's what the boss was having. It was at this dinner that the RCMP member laid out a scenario to the target in which he told him that, "when there are bumps in the road, we get rid of them."

The whirlwind of activity ended on May 2, 2001, in New Westminster, where the suspect was interviewed by Mr. Big, the head of the criminal empire that had been his employer for the preceding month. The suspect confided that he had killed the first victim because he had been bullied and berated by him in the past. Then he killed the landlord who lived next door because he was aware that his first victim had just paid cash for his rent. The suspect torched the residences and then walked up the hill, sat down and watched the houses burn. On May 3 we arrested the suspect at the Greyhound bus station in Chilliwack and charged him with the double murder.

Gloria Mott

At the same time that we were running the undercover operation for the Lillooet homicides, we used the same team of investigators to solve the case of Gloria Mott, who was murdered on the evening of December 25, 1982. On March 13, 2001, we made our first visual contact with the suspect as he emerged from his residence on Richards Street in downtown Vancouver. My surveillance team and I followed him throughout the afternoon as he meandered through the downtown core, picking cigarette butts out of public ashtrays.

By this time I had spent a considerable amount of my career conducting surveillance on criminals and had found that there are many difficult targets, the most difficult being the active organized-crime member, who constantly engages in counter-surveillance activity. While in the Drug Squad I had watched targets check the undersides of their vehicles, looking for tracking devices, then speed and run red lights to see if anybody followed. I have also seen higher-level criminals stop their vehicles in parking lots, get out with a pair of binoculars and try to locate surveillance aircraft. (I was in one of those aircraft at the time.) Other difficult subjects are drug traffickers (who always think they are being followed) and bank robbers who, prior to a robbery, go through an elaborate exercise to "clean" themselves of police surveillance.

People who are not particularly hard to follow are historical homicide suspects—unless they are still involved in criminal activity. The purpose of conducting surveillance on a homicide suspect is to give the undercover team a full package of information on the target's background in order to facilitate the initial contact and support the subsequent undercover activity. However, two of the targets I have followed and later arrested for murder had made the conscious decision to withdraw from the grid and were observed pushing shopping carts around their neighbourhoods, one in Vancouver's West End and the other in Port Coquitlam.

As part of the Mott investigation I interviewed Dan Savine, the first officer to attend the murder scene back in 1982—almost ten years earlier. Savine is both a good friend and a former colleague from my days in the Traffic Division. In the heyday of the Cold War, when the Soviets controlled most of Eastern Europe, Dan's mother had been in the Czech Air Force, and she had obtained travel documents from the socialist authorities so that she and her infant son could travel to Paris to attend a wedding. Documents in hand, they had then fled from France to Canada, where they became citizens. Dan, who is well over six feet tall, liked to tell the story of his second date with his wife, when she had mentioned that she had a black belt in karate. Laura is quite petite, and Dan considered her comment and then suggested that in the real world a black belt in karate wouldn't compensate for the substantial difference in their size and weight. When she disagreed, he took a fighter's stance and challenged, "Okay, why don't you show me what you've got?" Without hesitation, she executed a roundhouse kick to the side of Dan's head and knocked him to the ground. Then she ran and ran and ran.

As Dan is a pretty "heads-up" kind of policeman, I expected that he would have a fair recollection of the murder of Gloria Mott. His response came immediately. He recalled the crime scene as though he had been there yesterday and said, "It was Christmas Day, 1982 . . . afternoon shift. We killed two women that night."

He went on to describe how this had happened. At about dinnertime on December 25, Savine and his partner were called to the scene of a family dispute at 1729 Franklin Street on Vancouver's east side. When they arrived, they spoke to the victim, Gloria Mott, who had been beaten by her boyfriend. The suspect sported a small cut on his hand and said that Mott had attacked him. What the two agreed on was that the boyfriend had been watching television when Mott told him that Christmas dinner was ready. He said that he would eat when he finished watching television. Some discussion followed and Mott pulled the television cord out of the wall and cut it in two with a pair of scissors. The fight was on, and in the ensuing melee Mott was beaten and the boyfriend sustained a small cut to his hand. Following the policy and training of the day, Savine and his partner separated the combatants, offered counselling and advised the male to leave and cool off. He left, as did Savine and his partner.

A short time later on that same evening, Savine and his partner stopped a car for speeding on the Granville Street Bridge. Normally the driver of a vehicle stopped on the bridge will continue travelling off the bridge and then pull over where it is safe to do so. This one stopped about mid-point, and because the visibility was so good in either direction, the constables decided that the simplest way of dealing with the offender would be to put on their emergency lights, write a quick ticket and then be on their way. While they were dealing with the speeder in the darkness, a few hundred metres away on the downslope of the bridge, a jaywalking female pedestrian was hit and killed by a motorist who was distracted by the flashing lights of the police car.

Savine was still on the scene of this fatal motor vehicle accident when the police radio advised him there was now a party standing in front of the Franklin Street address, covered in blood. He and his partner returned to the scene to find Mott dead, her head smashed in by a hammer. The suspect (and previous antagonist) again claimed self-defence. No witnesses and a lack of evidence to the contrary resulted in no charges being laid.

Our undercover operation began on May 29, 2001, when the suspect agreed to assist the undercover officer in locating a female family member, now apparently on drugs and frequenting unsavory premises in the Downtown Eastside. The operator told the suspect that he could not go into the bars himself because the female would recognize him and flee. Flush with Mountie cash and with the photograph of the woman in hand, the suspect attended several taverns, searching for her.

I suggested that one of the suspect's future missions should be to conduct the "drop-the-dime scenario" at the Rose & Crown Pub in Tsawwassen. The drop-the-dime scenario involved having the target cover a meeting between his handler and another RCMP undercover member. The task given to the target is to note whether or not the undercover member makes a call from the bar as a result of the meeting. I once asked a group of young undercover operators why this ruse was called the "drop-the-dime scenario," and none of them had any idea. They were astounded to learn that the price of phone calls from public telephones used to be ten cents. Similarly, in the old gangster movies, when somebody "dropped a dime," it meant that they phoned the police to report criminal activity. Colloquially it means ratting out a criminal, usually by phone, to the police.

Another scenario that we involved this suspect in was the importation and subsequent sale of machine guns, which were tested at a range near Kelowna. Confidential arrangements were made with the president of the gun club, who authorized the use of the range and provided a key. Unfortunately, one of the range officers was not notified, and living within earshot of the property, he rushed to the scene (and sound) of the illegal gunfire, demanding an explanation. The crew beat a hasty retreat, while the cover team and I drove over to identify ourselves and explain that no further police intervention would be needed.

While the suspect was being run all over the province on his simulated crime spree, I participated in covering the various meetings and scenarios and writing up a Part VI warrant, which would allow audio and video recording of all subsequent meetings with the suspect and our undercover members. Until this warrant was granted, we monitored the conversations under the aegis of "one party consent" that was given by the sender or receiver of conversations (in this case, the undercover RCMP member), but this was done to ensure the safety of the officer and was usually not admissible in court. Writing up warrants is generally considered one of the most complicated, time-consuming and stressful tasks associated with working major-crime case files because some warrants contain hundreds of pages of information. Although not every aspect of evidence has to be contained in the Information to Obtain a Warrant (ITO), all relevant and germane information must be included. I was speaking to Crown counsel in her office in New Westminster about this particular warrant when one of my RCMP team members went staggering past, arms loaded with reams and reams of paper and documents. When Crown asked him, "What is that?" he responded, "It's my Information to Obtain a Warrant for one of our files." She shook her head and said, "Well, I'm not reading it, so take it away." He looked at me as though I should be able to intervene, but I gave him the "your battle, not mine" look.

There have been many books written to outline the nature of search warrants in an effort to streamline their preparation. Given that the officer (affiant) acts in good faith, the courts have been fairly forgiving regarding deficiencies, stating, "the ultimate question is not whether the ITO was long or poorly drafted, but rather whether it does, in fact, contain within it sufficient grounds upon which the search warrants could be issued," (Rafferty, M.T.C.S.; [paras 23-24] OSCJ) and "it would be impractical to expect of an officer swearing an information in these circumstances the precise prose of an Oxford grammarian, the detailed disclosures of a confessional and the legal knowledge of a Rhodes scholar" (Melenchuk, R; BCCA).

I found that I could write up a comprehensive ITO in about seventy-five pages, and other than the fact that writing up the document was time-consuming, I didn't think crafting one was as onerous as others seemed to. On several occasions I volunteered (assigned myself) for the task. To me, writing up an ITO relating to a murder was just like writing a really interesting story, the only real difference being that every minute detail had to be sourced back to the facts of the case. For example, in the preamble the author doesn't just identify himself as a police officer, he must describe his background and even how it came to pass that he became responsible for writing up the warrant.

Meanwhile, our undercover operation was going very well. It was explained to the target that his past, while of no interest to his new employer, was something that would have to be dealt with because the "Organization" was not home to individuals who brought unwelcome police attention. By mid-August 2001, our suspect had become fully involved in the undercover program and understood the importance of coming clean to Mr. Big, who would take whatever steps were necessary to erase his inconvenient past. This might include breaking into the police evidence locker and destroying all incriminating material, paying someone else to make a false confession or creating a rock solid alibi.

There were two issues critical to the suspect's confession to Mr. Big. The first was that he had to clearly understand that he could walk away from the crime family, no harm no foul. This is because investigators must be able to show in the clearest possible terms (captured via audio-video recording) that the suspect was not coerced and threatened into making a statement. So this was the focus of the first part of Mr. Big's preamble, and it was reinforced throughout the interview/confession. The suspect was also advised that the crime family's only request, should he walk away from them, was that he not disclose its existence to others. The second thing that is critical to such confessions is that the suspect has to disclose information that could only be known by the murderer, because investigators have to be able to show that he is not just parroting information that has been told to him by somebody else or that he has read or seen in the media. This is why modern investigators hold back some information relating to a murder from the public; then, when a suspect ultimately confesses, he can give up facts known to the murderer. However, in some investigations no information has been held back, and in these cases it is important to have the suspect completely convince Mr. Big (and the jury) that he is truly responsible for the crime by detailing all of the minutiae he can recall as well as his motivation, including his remorse or lack of it.

On August 23 the suspect, acting on his own initiative, and quite to the astonishment of all of us, walked through the front doors of the police station at 312 Main Street and told the front-counter staff that he wanted to confess to the murder of Gloria Mott. This move wasn't in the program. My old partner from the Robbery Squad, Detective Tim Eiger, attended the public information counter and took a comprehensive statement. The suspect was charged, escorted across the street to the provincial holding cells and was ultimately convicted of the murder. It was a minor diversion from the program, but it still goes up on the one-for-our-team scoreboard.

When investigating historical homicides, detectives can now use all of the modern tools available to solve the cases, although the most useful is DNA evidence, which can even be taken from a fingerprint that was left at the scene. However, the reality is that most of the modern advances only offer circumstantial evidence that pretty much requires corroboration, most desirably by confession. But while the numerous technical advances now buttress historical crime investigations, the weaknesses still include witnesses' loss of memory and the loss or destruction of exhibits.

I have found that the most comprehensive homicide packages reside in the dusty storage rooms of RCMP detachment offices, because generally when the initial investigation was over, the whole investigation was over. All of the evidence was packed up in cardboard boxes, which were taped up and shelved intact, awaiting the arrival of our investigators. With the VPD, an old homicide file would reside in at least three different locations. The investigative log itself would be filed in the records section, the fingerprint file with the Forensic Identification Unit, and the property itself at the property office—three different locations that must be individually canvassed by follow-up investigators.

The Murder of Ethan Hughes
On October 23, 2001, I flew to Prince Rupert to review the 1999 murder of Ethan Hughes, a small child who had been beaten to death while a family acquaintance, Jim Strachan was babysitting. The evidence revealed that the last witness to see the child alive was a visitor to the residence, who watched Ethan eating macaroni and watching cartoons on television. It was determined that there had been no other persons on the premises between the time the visitor left and a short while later when the suspect said he found the child in distress.

Ethan died of blunt force trauma so severe his esophagus had been detached from his stomach. The autopsy revealed that the macaroni was lodged in his stomach, so the beating took place after he had eaten. The suspect was arrested, made no statement to the police and was subsequently released, as the circumstantial case was not conclusive. The Prince Rupert detachment was asking for assistance in an effort to bring charges against the suspect, who was now living in the Lower Mainland. The investigation of this murder, which had taken place barely two years earlier, was stretching the mandate of the Historical Homicide Unit, but the innocence of the victim was compelling motivation. I attended the Prince Rupert detachment office, picked up the file and loaded it into the trunk of my Mountie loaner car, then returned to my hotel room and did a file review. It was pretty straightforward. The next morning I met with the Prince Rupert officers and we discussed possible avenues to move the investigation along. They were in favour of wire-tapping the suspect's phone, then staging a scenario that would cause him to believe arrest and a charge were imminent, thus provoking him to phone some as yet unknown confidant to get advice. I didn't buy it. With a crime as despicable as this one, it was not likely that the incident would come up in conversation, regardless of police inducement. I didn't think that there was anything that could be done to motivate the suspect to discuss the issue with a confidant in person or on the phone. It was not the kind of crime that a person would admit to.

I explained how the undercover program operated and committed the resources of the Unsolved Homicide Unit to an investigation that would take three or four months. For the first month or so I would do a lifestyle investigation (the initial investigation into a target prior to the insertion of the undercover team) into the behaviour of the target, Jim Strachan, followed by the introduction of the undercover team who would run a Mr. Big scenario. They seemed surprised by the level of commitment that was being offered but supported my strategy because it made sense and also because the Provincial Unit would be picking up the tab. The Prince Rupert investigator volunteered to write the Information to Obtain a Warrant and the Crown Counsel Report.

I had decided that since the suspect was a country mouse now living in the city, I could handle the initial surveillance myself. On October 26 I drove to a residence on 49th Avenue in Vancouver, just west of Boundary Road, set up so that I had a view of the front door and waited to see whether or not the suspect was truly on-site. There was no activity and no suggestion that the house was inhabited. On October 29 I re-attended the area and again set up with a view of the front door. At 3:45 p.m. a male wearing glasses came out of the lane beside the house, walked north, then headed across Boundary Road and east on Imperial Street to a bookstore, where he bought a videotape. He was in the store for only a few minutes before he exited and walked back to his residence. I gave the Prince Rupert investigator a call and confirmed that Strachan did, in fact, wear glasses.

On October 31 I met with Don Amberson, the staff sergeant in charge of the Historical Homicide Unit, and went over my operational plan for the Hughes investigation. Amberson was one of the most effective supervisors I ever worked for; his decisions were based on rock-solid logic, he made them instantly and he had the backing of the Senior Management Team. Once I had a discussion with him regarding changes he had made to budget guidelines for overtime and told him I didn't really understand how the changes were going to be implemented. He mulled it over for a moment, and then said, "Well, don't worry about it. These changes don't apply to you. I like the way you deal with overtime."

On this occasion we discussed the dynamic of the Hughes investigation and concerns that the undercover unit was not going to be available anytime soon. When we concluded the meeting, he commented that he didn't like to see his people writing reports for the sake of writing reports and added, "So you can tell Vancouver that they can take their monthly reports and shove them up their ass." I asked, "Did you want me to temper that a bit?" He responded, "You can tell them any way you want to, but we are not going to send them any more monthly reports updating them on the progress of our investigations."

It was now my task to inform the inspector in charge of Vancouver's Homicide Unit that the RCMP had decided that he could shove his monthly reports up his ass. The new inspector in charge of that unit was my old classmate and Strike Force partner Christopher Shore. I attended his office to reminisce about our Cushman Clown Car racing days and pass along the staff sergeant's decision.

Christopher Shore and I were both thankful to the RCMP for ending the worthless exercise of writing a monthly report and were loudly laughing and guffawing about the old days when spontaneously and without warning, his new forty-pound computer monitor (not one of the sleek and light modern ones), which had been perched on a high shelf, crashed from its place, smashed onto the desk right beside me, then bounced onto the floor, taking with it files, books, pens and assorted police collectables. The Major Crime bullpen is located immediately outside of his office and none of the detectives working there had any idea about our friendship. What they would have heard was loud emotional voices, followed by the smashing of large furniture. We were trying to straighten the shelf and set the broken monitor back on it, causing even more noise, when there was a knock on the door, and we heard one of the detectives (no doubt chosen by short straw) ask, "Is everything all right in there?" I suggested that the play here would be to simulate a fight, but logic and common sense prevailed.

Between October 29, 2001, and February 11, 2002, I completed a fairly rock-solid background investigation of Jim Strachan. Although in the beginning I had done the surveillance myself, as the timeline to the insertion of the undercover team drew closer, other members of my team worked with me. We had learned that Strachan was working at a construction site in the 6800 block of Station Hill Drive in South Burnaby, where his job was installing large glass windows on a new high-rise building. At this point I asked the Prince Rupert investigator to attend our location for the initial bump between Strachan and Constable Jim Elder, our undercover operator.

On February 12, our team set up to contain Strachan's residence. At 7:30 a.m. he came out of the carport of his residence wearing a lumberman's jacket, a white hard hat and carrying a backpack. He walked to the Edmonds SkyTrain Station and caught the eastbound train to his worksite. At 5:45 p.m. Strachan left the job site and headed home. As he walked away from the Edmonds Station along Central Boulevard, I pulled out of my location with Constable

Foreman (the Prince Rupert RCMP investigator) sitting beside me. Elder was pulled over to the side of the road and talking to Strachan at the driver's door. As we drove past the undercover vehicle, Foreman covered her face so Strachan wouldn't recognize her. They had met two years earlier when she arrested him for the murder. Almost four months had passed since I started investigating the case, and now we had the initial investigator on hand to witness first contact between Constable Elder and the target.

By February 15 the operation was underway and Strachan had been tasked with checking bars throughout the Lower Mainland in an effort to locate a runaway family member. In the course of the first few scenarios Strachan seemed suspicious and unnaturally reluctant to participate in the short, simple and relatively lucrative scenarios he was involved in. When quizzed about his skepticism, he told Elder (and there is of course no way of knowing whether or not this is true) that an advisor had told him that, in the case of a serious crime he was suspected of committing, the police simply didn't have enough evidence to support a charge. This advisor had added that as time went by, he might meet a new friend and that person would introduce him to a criminal empire. Ultimately, in the course of participating in that criminal lifestyle he would be required to confess to the murder so that the new crime family would make all of the evidence and the suspicions relating to it go away. All of these new people and the empire itself would be instruments of the RCMP, who fabricated the operation in order to obtain a confession. "So," Strachan told Elder, "You can see why I was a little suspicious at first, but now I can see that you are solid guys."

On April 23 Elder and Strachan were on the way to a debt collection when, as planned, they were stopped on

Great Northern Way by a marked police car. It was driven by a friend of mine, Vancouver Police Sergeant Tony Zanatta (who had volunteered). Zanatta commented to Elder, loudly enough for Strachan to hear, that Strachan was a suspect in a murder investigation. Elder was shocked to hear such a thing.

Tony Zanatta's family had a history in policing, and he once told me how his father had influenced the way he treated people. Back in the 1940s Antonio Zanatta (Tony Senior) had been a policeman in Genoa, Italy, but at the end of the war, after Mussolini was executed, partisans drove around the countryside rounding up anybody who was thought to be a Fascist collaborator. A car full of partisans with sub-machine guns pulled up beside Tony and his partner, who were in uniform and by virtue of their office now deemed to be enemies of the state. They were disarmed, ordered into the trunk of the car and delivered to the graveyard.

The partisans had rounded up five people in all and ordered them up against a wall. Then one of the leaders approached Tony and asked him his name. He said, "I remember you. You treated me well." It seems that one day when he had been out on foot patrol, he had arrested the man for stealing. As there were no phones, the fellow requested that Tony go with him to his house so that he could tell his mother he was going to jail. They took a bus to the house, and Tony stayed while the mother prepared a meal for him and her son. When they finished eating, Tony and his prisoner took a bus to the police station. The man reminisced about their previous encounter for a few minutes, then pulled Tony out of the line. "No, not this one. He treated me fairly. You can go! Run!" As Tony's father ran from the graveyard, he heard the sub-machinegun fire. The next day the local authorities collected four bodies.

On April 24 I arrived early at a hotel near the airport to help set up the equipment of "Special I," the RCMP unit that deals with electronic monitoring and surveillance. We had a room adjoining the one that Mr. Big was going to use for his interview with Strachan so that we could run hard wire between the camera and the recording devices that we would be monitoring. Because of the close proximity, we had to be careful about the noise we were making as well as the smell of popcorn, which might reveal our presence while we watched the live performance going on in the next room via a video screen. One would think that in these modern times the whole process could be handled wirelessly, and Special I does, in fact, have all the equipment to do that. The problem is that they can't guarantee that, should the suspect turn the TV on to a specific channel, he won't be watching himself being recorded. Hardwiring the system still offers the best recording quality.

When you are running these scenarios, it is hard to believe that the hotel, especially an upscale one, isn't aware that something nefarious is going on. They see a lot of big guys with tattoos and long hair who other than that seem awfully healthy and clean, and these guys bring a lot of equipment with them and want adjoining rooms. In a small town our guys pretend to be scouting for a new location for an IKEA or a similar store. In the big city they can make up anything to explain their presence, but it still is hard to believe that hotel management doesn't know that something is up.

In this case, we had just popped the ceiling panels between the two rooms and were running cables between the camera and the recorders, which passed near the door of the suite, when I heard a knock on the door. I leaned up against the door as the porter called: "Room service!" Not hearing a response, he opened the door with his key. I stopped it from opening wide, but it was still a few inches ajar as he asked me a question about the reservation. I answered and shut the door, but I knew he must have noticed the bails of rolled wire hanging from the ceiling panel above me. Thankfully, nothing came of it.

That night Strachan confessed to Mr. Big and described the beating he gave the child by holding up a couch pillow to demonstrate. On May 13, 2002, I coordinated the attendance of an arrest team to Waverly Avenue and Imperial Street in Burnaby, where Strachan had been located at a 7-Eleven store. He was taken into custody, and I attended with badge in hand to serve him with the formal arrest warrant that had been sworn by the Prince Rupert RCMP for the murder of Ethan Hughes. The video recording of Strachan confessing the specific details of the crime was so compelling that he was found guilty at trial.

Grave Robbers

In early February 2001 I spoke to the coroner about a case where a woman was attempting to locate her brother, who had been missing since 1987. In that same era an unidentified male had been buried at the Carman United Church Cemetery in Chilliwack, and the sister was convinced that this male and her brother were one and the same, that there had been foul play, and she had a suspect in mind. Discussion ensued and we decided that there was a possibility that the grave did, in fact, hold the remains of her vanished sibling. In any case, we could take some DNA from the remains in an effort to determine identity.

On February 25 I called my brother to see if he was busy the next day. Hearing that he was not, I told him to meet me at the cemetery at three the following afternoon and to bring a shovel. (Come on! Who in their right mind would miss an opportunity to stand at the bottom of a grave, scraping out a skeleton, bone by bone, to further a homicide investigation?) The site manager used a little bulldozer on rubber tracks that didn't disturb the other grassy plots in order to get down to the collapsed wooden casket. We did the rest of the exhumation by hand, placing the remains in a heavy, black plastic body bag.

On March 4 I went to the morgue at Royal Columbian Hospital in New Westminster with the coroner and a physical anthropologist from Simon Fraser University for an examination of the remains. As I walked into the morgue, a couple of RCMP investigators were just opening a suitcase that had been taken from Pitt Lake. Inside were the remains of a small Asian girl. She looked very tranquil and there were no overt indicators to suggest the cause of death. As I went over to our gurney, a staff pathologist was finishing up with a body at another table. A third table was in use by another doctor who was about halfway through an examination.

I listened to the anthropologist, who had recently been working on a war crimes investigation for the United Nations. It was all darkly interesting stuff about the carnage that ensued after civilians had hidden in a well and combatants had tossed grenades down upon them. Unfortunately, a local change of government had made the results much less interesting to the new regime, and funding for the investigation had been withdrawn. As he methodically catalogued the bones we had recovered, the first pathologist rolled in another body and started anew.

I thought that this was going to be a pretty busy Monday morning. One exhumation, one murdered girl in a suitcase and three standard autopsies. It was a record for me. Not too long into our examination, the anthropologist advised that the subject in our case had been at least fifty years old, though probably much older. That was it, far too old to be our missing person, so I left the remains with the coroner and the woman's brother remained missing.

Vancouver's Centrefold Murders

In 1981, while I had been a firearms instructor at the Justice Institute, I had attended every interesting course or lecture that was offered at the Institute, and one that stood out in my mind over the years was a fascinating presentation given by lead detective Jim Stone to regional investigators in the hope of spurring their interest or insight into Vancouver's "Centrefold Murders."

A year earlier, in November 1980, there had been a double murder at a rooming house on Cambridge Street in East Vancouver. Eldon Jacobs and Marilyn Meersman had been stabbed many times in the course of an apparent robbery. In the macabre crime, Meersman's body had been positioned with an open umbrella. Next to the female victim was a copy of the May 1979 issue of Playboy magazine, open at the centrefold, which depicted a young model holding an umbrella in the same position.

Jacobs' van had been filled with things from the house and then driven west until it ran out of gas in a Downtown Eastside parking lot. A pop bottle on the floor on the passenger side was dusted and revealed a partial print; it was run through the police databases with negative results. A psychological profiler from the FBI evaluated the crime and determined that the killer was probably older, quiet, a loner and an outdoorsman. The investigators found that a tenant fitting that profile had been recently evicted from the rooming house. That former tenant, Werner Hoffman, immediately became the prime suspect and was taken into custody. While he promptly and decisively failed the polygraph examination, polygraph cannot be used as evidence in court, and there was no confession. So with no hard evidence against the suspect, he was released. It was an extraordinary case.

More than two decades later, on June 27, 2001, one of my team members who had been liaising with the Vancouver Police Identification Squad was told that a person of interest had surfaced relative to the Centrefold Murders. The fingerprint taken from the pop bottle left in the stolen vehicle had been cleaned up and re-submitted to the federal database, and a hit had come back identifying the print as belonging to Michael Rayson. This was enough to trigger a file review. In an effort to locate evidence, the detective attended the VPD Property Office on June 28 and 29 and July 12, only to be told that all of the evidence relating to the case had been destroyed.

Unlike some television comedies that can be a show about nothing, a homicide case has to be a show about something. A murder investigation cannot be based on just a distant memory, a clipping from a newspaper or a report in a file. There must be physical evidence relating to the crime—a weapon, the victim's clothing, something seized from the scene. It can be anything, but it has to be something significant or there is no prosecution. So, in frustration, the detective brought the file to me, asking for an opinion about a case that had gone terminal. We decided that I would take over the investigation. The detective ended his logbook for the homicide investigation on September 17, 2001, and I started mine.

Eldon Jacobs and Marilyn Meersman had lived in a rooming house on Cambridge Street in company with Jimmy Cove and Werner Hoffman. Jacobs, who was gay, was a huge, six-foot-five, gregarious man, but he was also argumentative, particularly when drinking. His part of the house was crowded with the knickknacks he had collected, and he was in charge of collecting rent from the others for the landlord. Meersman was a new tenant and a longtime platonic friend of Jacobs. A legal secretary who got along well with everybody, she had recently moved to Vancouver and was not expected to stay at the residence for more than a few months. Jimmy Cove was a bit of a wild man, and when the murders occurred, he had been partying all night (and for the previous two days) with friends. Cove and Jacobs had known each other for about fifteen years, both having come from the same neighbourhood in Edmonton, where they had frequented a small café called the Java Shop. Werner Hoffman, an older man who spoke with a European accent, was an avid salmon fisherman. Although a longtime tenant, he had become the victim of a younger demographic, and after he complained about the other tenants' excessive noise on a number of occasions, Jacobs told him to pack up and leave. It is said that the squeaky wheel gets the grease, but it can also often be the first one to be replaced.

Hoffman said that he had last seen Jacobs at the residence on Monday, November 10, 1980, between noon and 1 p.m., when he handed over his keys and asked that his mail be delivered to his new address. Twenty-two years later, on October 21, 2002, he remembered to tell follow-up investigators that when he handed over the keys, there had been a younger man on the premises. Initial investigators had spoken to the owner of the house, who told them that he was out of town on the week of November 12, but when he spoke to Jacobs on November 9, Jacobs told him that he had a friend from Edmonton staying over. As Meersman had only been living at the house a short while, the implication had been that Jacobs was talking about her.

On November 10 Jacobs had driven his van to a gas station that was run by a friend in order to borrow some money. The friend later told investigators he knew there was a passenger in the front seat, maybe a kid, who Jacobs spoke to, but he couldn't describe this person. Years later, when I drew Detective Stone's attention to the information relating to this unknown party in the van at 2:30 p.m. on November 10, 1980, he said, "We didn't have any suspects other than Hoffman except the kid, and that appeared to be a homosexual pickup by Eldon, and it seemed like that was a one-night-stand thing."

At about 2 p.m. on November 11, 1980, Cove phoned Jacobs from the home of a friend in Coquitlam, where he had been drinking for about five days, and asked if there had been any mail for him from Edmonton. Jacobs said that everything was okay but complained that gold prices were down so he had to sell some off and that he was going to have a few drinks. Jacobs was purportedly a bullion trader and his daily routine was to phone his bank to enquire about gold and silver prices. Prone to exaggerating his wealth, Jacobs had told Cove that he was the owner of the house on Cambridge Street as well as two other condominiums.

In the early hours of November 12, 1980, neighbours said they heard a vehicle being revved again and again beside Jacobs' residence. The vehicle seemed to move a short distance, stop and have to be restarted. At 2:30 p.m. on that same day, Cove returned to his residence to pick up his mail. Three friends waited in the car while Cove used his key to unlock the front door and enter the house. He could see that the hallway had been disturbed, and a lot of things were missing. Jacobs' trench coat was not on the chair in the entryway where it was always draped, and the door leading to the kitchen was open, which was unusual. There was a mess in the kitchen. "The spice rack had been pulled off the wall, there was tea and coffee all over the place." He entered and discovered Jacobs' body lying on its back in a sitting room that was next to the kitchen.

Cove went back to the three friends waiting in the vehicle and asked them to come in and have a look. They refused, so he went back into the house, picked up his jeans, sweaters and a hat from his room and noticed that his suitcase was missing. Then he drove over to the police station to report what he had found. On his way there he noticed that the clothing he had taken from the house, including his hat, had been doused in what he called a "burning oil," and he recalled that, when he was taking his clothing from his room, there had been a can of this scented oil on his desk. Investigators later considered that the culprit had planned to use the oil as an accelerant to torch the crime scene but for some reason had not followed through.

Two Vancouver police constables arrived at the scene at approximately 3 p.m. and noted that there was no sign of forced entry. Half an hour later a Homicide Unit team, which included Detective Tim Stone, arrived. They found Jacobs lying on his back; he was wearing jeans, a blue t-shirt and an orange and blue flowered shirt. His face had been mutilated and there were numerous stab wounds to his chest. Strangely, a smashed birdcage was lying across his chest, which was covered with birdseed and soaked with blood. There were feathers strewn across his face. It appeared that there had been quite a struggle, as there was blood on the lower portion of the wall and floor, indicating that at some point the body had been dragged across the room. There was some lasagna in an aluminum container on the stove, which was turned off, cupboards were open and spice bottles smashed. There were two empty vodka bottles on the floor. In the living room, investigators found a broken fish tank, which still had its lights on. The area had been trashed, and the dead bird from the smashed cage was found in a cardboard box containing firewood.

Upstairs, a broken clock was found on the hall floor beside Marilyn Meersman's room. The time showed 12:31. The detectives found her dead in her bedroom. Her body was on a mattress under a pink blanket. Removing the blanket, the investigators saw that she had on a pink nightdress and a red and pink dressing gown, but these garments only covered her upper arms and shoulders. Meersman had been stabbed once in the back, and many times in the front, and arranged with an open umbrella and Playboy magazine. Numerous articles in the room were thrown about, and ink was splattered over the mess.

The door to Jacobs' upstairs bedroom had been kicked in, the doors to unlocked cupboards had been torn off their hinges and the room ransacked. Cove's bedroom door had been unlocked but it, too, was kicked open, and some of his things were thrown around the room. The door to Hoffman's upstairs bedroom was also kicked in, and investigators found a box spring and mattress lying on their sides, but the room was comparatively clean. There was a garlic sausage and a partial bottle of wine in Hoffman's fridge. In the upstairs bathroom, the ceramic toilet lid had been turned upside down. A black floral shirt soaking in the bathtub had stains on it that investigators thought could have been blood. Because of smudging throughout the crime scene, detectives believed that the culprit had worn gloves.

At 6:40 p.m. Jacobs' van was located in the parking lot of the Drake Hotel in the 600 block of Powell Street, twenty blocks from 2580 Cambridge Street; it had apparently run out of gas. The van's battery was dead; its keys were discovered in the glovebox. In the van were a suitcase full of property, a guitar, a .303 rifle, a typewriter, a camera, various items of men's clothing and a large wooden chest containing numerous stereo components, all stolen from the house. A pop bottle was found on the floor between the seats, and a police report indicated that it "appeared to have been put there recently." A Fairbairn-Sykes commando knife in its sheath was stuffed between the back and bottom of the driver's seat. The knife appeared to have blood on its hilt, and Detective Stone attended to note that the measurements and configuration of the blade were consistent with the wounds found on the bodies. In the vehicle were a pair of grey woolen gloves, which appeared to have blood on the finger areas. The van was staked out for twelve hours and then towed into the police compound lot.

Only one print of interest was found in the van. This was on the pop bottle. In my follow-up investigation twenty years after the crime, I asked the Identification Unit member why he had thought the pop bottle had been placed there recently, and he answered, "because it was spotlessly clean" and the floor was dirty. He could not remember whether the bottle had been standing up or lying on its side when the police located the van. This would have been the best affirmation of its recent use, as it would suggest that the driver had placed the bottle on the floor after the van was parked. The fingerprint was run through the national database with negative result. However, one of the fingerprint technicians left a copy of the print on his desk for years, saying, "When that print comes in, we'll have him." And then in June 2001 that print was identified.

The Suspects

Jimmy Cove had been partying with friends at the time of the murders. In any case, he took and passed a polygraph examination. Ronald Black, Meersman's ex-husband and a friend of Jacobs, stated that he was at work, then at home with his brother and sister-in-law at the time of the murders. He also took and passed a polygraph.

Werner Hoffman was arrested on November 19 and placed in the Vancouver police cells with an undercover officer. There he made some astounding comments: he asked his cellmate, "Does it make any difference if you kill more than one person?" and "Could I get anything more if, say, I killed more than one person, like maybe two or three?" Ten or fifteen times during the night, he asked, "If you were in my shoes and you were a hundred percent sure you didn't do it, would you plead guilty or not guilty?" And he told his cellmate, "The worst thing is when you have to face rejection from a woman. You know, you make a play for one and she thinks she is too good for you."

Hoffman was given a polygraph examination and registered a number of deceptive responses. When I later interviewed the polygrapher, he told me, "It was clear in the course of the polygraph examination that he was guilty of the offence. He broke down in the pretest, saying something about a vision from God." At one point the examiner had thought he was going to have to call in another officer because of Hoffman's erratic behaviour, but as they had no specific admission of guilt from him, the police released Hoffman, though they placed him under surveillance. No incriminating evidence was subsequently found.

When I asked Stone who the principal suspect was, he said, "It was Hoffman. We didn't have any other suspects but the kid, and that went nowhere." Stone, an avid fisherman, then mentioned that he used to fish the Vedder River in the Fraser Valley. On several occasions he found himself fishing in proximity to Hoffman and would hurl accusations across the river at him. Hoffman would yell back, "I didn't do it!"

Michael Rayson, whose fingerprint was matched to that pop bottle in the van, twenty years after the crime, had been seventeen years old at the time of the murders. Today, he would be considered a juvenile, but back then, if the evidence had supported a charge, he would have been dealt with as an adult. He had convictions for more than twenty offences, ranging from his first, which was committing mischief and injuring or endangering animals (Fort Saskatchewan, Alberta, May 7, 1980) to drug possession (Surrey, 2000). Tracking the locations of his offences showed that Rayson had moved from Edmonton to Vancouver in 1984. I was particularly interested in the charge concerning injuring animals, because the two murders in the Cambridge Street house just six months later had involved the killing of a bird and some fish. I have reviewed hundreds and hundreds of criminal records and cannot recall one incident (except for the case of flamingo-cide in Stanley Park) where an accused party had been convicted of animal cruelty.

On October 2, 2001, I attended the Property Office at 312 Main Street and spoke to one of the managers there in an effort to determine what had happened to the evidence in this case. At that time evidence was stored off-site in a crowded, dusty old building several blocks from the main police station. Although I knew it had been standard practice in those days for property to be disposed of when major-crime files were closed, I also knew it was standard practice to have an investigator sign off on that destruction. But all of the detectives on this case were long retired, so I couldn't understand why the evidence was gone.

Out came the logbooks relating to the file—old stained tomes full of notations, signatures, initials and hieroglyphics that only Property Office staff could really understand. I was told conclusively that all of the evidence had been destroyed. The Playboy magazine, the knife, the umbrella, the clothing, the clock . . . everything, all of it was gone. I thought that this was going to be the shortest investigation I had ever done. I left the building in disbelief.

Then, on the morning of October 4, I phoned the property office and spoke again to the clerk who had earlier presented me with the property log. I advised him that I was concluding the file, but first I wanted to go over all of the logbook entries with him, and I wanted him to decipher the notations for me so I could add that information to my final report. I asked if he could set aside time for me later that morning, as I was a bit thick and the property management protocols seemed awfully complicated. No problem, he said. He would clear his desk for later that morning.

At 11:45 I attended the property office and spoke to the clerk, who already had the property books out in anticipation of my arrival. I told him that I did want him to interpret that information for me, but first I wanted him to take me to the property garage and show me specifically where evidence from homicides of that era were lodged. He explained that the cases weren't catalogued that way, and there were literally thousands of parcels of evidence at that location. Besides, the log said that in this case, all of it had been destroyed. I told him that I understood completely, but that I wanted him to humour me, even if it was a waste of a few hours.

We drove the four blocks to the building, which he unlocked by key and security pad. Inside there were rows and rows of racks full of dusty boxes, envelopes and packages. I thought: this is going to be impossible. Then I asked him, "Okay, you know it's a homicide from 1980, and I'm looking for a knife, an umbrella, some documents and all kinds of other evidence that isn't necessarily in a box. So you are the expert here. Let's say that the evidence is here somewhere, anywhere. Where would you look?"

"It's not here," he said.

"I understand that completely," I said, "but if it were here, where would you look?"

He sighed, relenting, and escorted me to a set of opposing racks about twelve metres long and two and a half metres high that contained boxes and file folders and large envelopes. "This would be my best guess," he said.

I started opening each unsealed box and pushed aside stacks of evidence, envelopes and loose, tagged property that had been there for decades. I spent about forty-five minutes jostling and shifting the dusty containers around, thinking that this would probably take a couple of days. Then I moved one storage box that was on a shelf at about chest level. Wedged between it and the next box was a very large manila property envelope with an umbrella handle sticking out of it. Inside the envelope, along with the umbrella, was the broken clock and some personal photos that had been collected from the crime scene. I held it up and just glared at the property clerk. But fair enough, he had actually helped me find the evidence I needed to make this a show about something.

I started looking for Rayson immediately. From his crime sheet, I knew he had bounced around the Lower Mainland over the course of the last fifteen years. On October 11 I set up surveillance on the Arco Hotel on West Pender Street in Vancouver but saw no activity. The next day a possible target exited and one of my detectives and I followed him as he wandered around the West End. We were unable to make a positive identification.

On January 10, 2002, I phoned the Fort Saskatchewan RCMP to request that they research the particulars regarding the charges against Rayson. I was told that in minor cases all information is purged after five years and there was nothing on file relating to the conviction. Frustrated by my inability to positively identify the man, I spoke to Tony Zanatta (yes, him again) and asked that he attend the Arco Hotel to check for my suspect. On January 24 Zanatta knocked on the door of room 509 and it was answered by a male person who identified himself as Monty Grayson and gave a birthdate two and half years younger than the target. But Zanatta positively identified this party as Rayson from a photo I had given him.

Meanwhile, the Provincial Unsolved Homicide Unit was gearing up to tackle the Missing Women's file, and on March 5, 2002, all of the sergeants at the Unsolved Homicide Unit were called in for a meeting with Staff Sergeant Amberson. "Project Evenhanded" was being initiated and all other investigations, except my Prince Rupert file, were being put on hold. As Amberson started describing how he was looking for a project leader, I started backing my chair toward the door. This was going to be a massive investigation, and I was already in the middle of an undercover operation, but I volunteered to assist if any breaks in my schedule occurred. One of the few contributions I made to the "Evenhanded" file was to interview the suspect's (Robert "Willie" Pickton's) friends. I did one these interviews in Port Coquitlam with one of Pickton's best friends, who told me, "If I would have known Willie was cutting up those girls, I would have put him on a tight leash . . . I would have shut him down."

"Do you think you would have called the police?" I asked.

"No. No, I don't think so." It was an interesting perspective.

I learned that Rayson would be attending provincial court at 222 Main Street on June 18, 2002, at 9 a.m. to deal with some charges, and I figured this would give me a chance to identify him close up. In fact, he sat right in front of me in the courtroom. I left the building immediately before he did and took up a position on Main Street. Following him south on Main, I watched him turn west onto Pender and followed him to his hotel. A short time later he left the Arco, having adopted a completely new persona. He was now dressed like a California surfer with Huaraches sandals and a Hawaiian shirt, though he was pushing a not-so-cool shopping cart. As he rolled through the West End, he collected bottles and recyclables, redeeming them at a shop on Davie Street. Between June 18 and October 8, 2002, I conducted surveillance on Rayson nine times, usually by myself. He spent his days picking through Dumpsters and seemed quite social as he interacted with other members of the "binner" subculture. Once he used his recycling cash to buy a bottle from a government liquor store near Bidwell Street and poured drinks for his friends as they enjoyed the sun on a bench in Alexandra Park overlooking English Bay.

On August 20 I had a meeting with Staff Sergeant Amberson and the other sergeants on the squad to give them an update on my investigation. I was having difficulty coordinating my interview with Detective Stone, now retired and living on Cortes Island off the BC Coast. When I explained that I would have to take three ferries and stay overnight at a bed and breakfast just to get to his residence, one of the other sergeants said, "Why don't you just take the RCMP helicopter?" He suggested it as though it were no different than calling for a cab. And I thought: That's right! Why don't I just take the RCMP helicopter? And apparently it was just as simple as calling for a cab. Notification that I was working on a homicide file and that transport was an operational necessity meant that I had the highest priority flight status. I was scheduled for an August 23 liftoff. We were early for the interview, so on the way over we GPS-marked some outdoor marijuana grow operations that we passed over. The crop shows up as a crystal-bright emerald colour that contrasts with the darker conifers of West Coast forests. As we flew north, the pilot transmitted the coordinates of these operations to ground units that would later attend to clear the crop with machetes and industrial brush cutters.

We landed on the helicopter pad at the Cortes Island firehall, and the pilot said he would return in three hours, after he had completed some more Drug Squad recon. As I got off of the helicopter, I was wearing a black suit and dark sunglasses and carrying a briefcase full of files. I was going for a man-in-black look (Tommy Lee Jones, not Johnny Cash) that I figured would keep the small community abuzz. At the firehall I unloaded my files and went over them with Stone,

who had a pretty good memory of the murders. He reaf-
firmed that Hoffman and "the kid" were the only suspects
who had ever surfaced in the case. As I awaited my air taxi
for the return, the receptionist at the desk joked, "You must
be important, having your own helicopter to drop you off
and pick you up." I responded stoically, "Ma'am, I'm not
important. The file is important." Cortes Island would be
talking about this for years.

Another of my interviews took place in one of Edmonton's more rundown neighbourhoods. Having had no luck
contacting a witness by phone, I rang the doorbell at an old
rooming house, hoping to locate a fellow who had been a
very close friend of Jacobs, Meersman and Cove immediately before the murders. My purpose was to get first-hand,
personal background information about the victims. An
unhealthy-looking, sallow man in his sixties answered the
door. I identified myself and briefly explained why I was
there. Though resistant at first, he reluctantly escorted me
down the threadbare-carpeted stairs to a dimly lit suite that
smelled of mould. I took off my shoes before entering his
room and left them on the rubber floor mat. He asked if I
would like some tea. I answered that I would have some, but
only if he was brewing it for himself. He told me that he had
spoken to a lot of police in the past and had generally refused
to cooperate in any way. Then he looked down at my stocking
feet and said, "You are the first one that has ever treated me
with any respect." He went on to offer a completely candid
and comprehensive recollection of the circumstances
surrounding the decades-old murder.

On August 26, after reflecting on my success with the
VPD property office, I phoned Fort Saskatchewan RCMP
again and spoke to another constable. I told him that, while

I understood the force had a five-year-purge policy written to discourage nuisance requests for old files, sometimes the files were not actually destroyed. Then I asked for the big favour. Would he mind walking across the street to the courthouse, kidnap a file clerk and then physically go to where the old files are kept in an effort to locate the record in question. "No problem," he said. He phoned back a short time later to exclaim, "We found it!" Michael Rayson. Count 1: On or about the 23rd day of April, 1980, at or near Fort Saskatchewan did willfully damage eggs and kill a bird, both of which were being held for a legal purpose. Bingo! We had a bird killer and a slam dunk for getting a warrant approval. I submitted an Operational Plan to conduct an undercover operation on Michael Rayson, which was approved and named "Project Elias."

The Undercover Operation
Over the course of the first few undercover operations I had been involved in, I had made it a priority to write up commendations for the officers involved, outlining their involvement and the role they had played in the investigation. I'd had no ulterior motive when writing up these citations, as the officers all deserved recognition, but it never occurred to me that I was the only one committing these thoughts to paper until one day when I was at a meeting with the undercover unit and I was introduced to one of these constables. He said, "Cope . . . you're the one that writes the letters." I was then told that when I sent a request for an undercover operation to their office, it was prioritized and sent to the top of the pile.

On October 3 I met with the RCMP Undercover Unit sergeant at the Provincial Unsolved Homicide Office in

Surrey to discuss strategy. We were now up and running. On October 8 I was out on foot, the RCMP sergeant and the undercover operator in vehicles, all of us searching the West End for the target. We had come to the end of the shift and we were just about ready to pack it up for the day and head back to the station. I began walking toward the sergeant's location two blocks away when I looked east, down the south lane of Davie, and saw Rayson pushing his shopping cart west toward Denman. I notified the team that the target was on his way, and quick work got Constable Elder to the scene for the first of many criminal scenarios. The shift went into overtime as Elder and Rayson drove around the Downtown Eastside, checking the seedier bars for the girl in the photo that Elder had shown him.

Between October 8 and December 4, 2002, Constable Elder engaged in thirteen scenarios with Rayson. He was hired to "watch Elder's back" as he engaged in simulated minor criminal activity, transported a suspicious package from the locker at one bus depot to another, then engaged in laundering $250,000 in counterfeit funds. When running a scenario dealing with counterfeit money, the usual script involves trading several hundred thousand dollars in counterfeit Canadian money for 20 percent of that value in American cash. So where do you dig up two or three hundred thousand dollars' worth of counterfeit money? You don't. All of the cash used is real, both Canadian and American. Other scenarios involved a criminal transaction related to the theft of a top-secret computer program, assisting with a debt collection and selling illegal firearms. Rayson was well paid for all of these jobs. And throughout this undercover operation he was instructed that the organization's guiding principles were truth, loyalty and honesty, these values being re-enforced again and again in the course of the undercover operation.

On December 5 at approximately 8:30 a.m., VPD Detective Spall attended the Arco Hotel and spoke with Rayson, advising that he was investigating two murders from 1980. Other than the fact that the murders took place on Cambridge Street in Vancouver and the victims were Eldon Jacobs and Marilyn Meersman, Spall offered no further information. He told Rayson that his name had surfaced in the course of the investigation and he wanted to set up a time when they could discuss the matter thoroughly. Rayson asked if he was being charged and was told he was not. Then Rayson said that he hadn't been in Vancouver in 1980 and didn't arrive to the city until 1984. Spall left a card asking Rayson to call him the following week to set up an appointment. This whole scenario was conducted to prompt Rayson into confiding about the crime with Elder.

On December 6 Rayson met with Elder and told him he was being investigated for a homicide that took place between 1980 and 1984. Rayson said he was drunk at the time the policeman talked to him at the Arco so he couldn't remember exactly what was said to him. He told Elder that he had been just fifteen years old in 1980 and that a year later, when he turned sixteen, he had moved out and existed surfing from couch to couch. In 1982 he had hitchhiked to San Francisco, then back to Edmonton. He said that he came out to Vancouver in 1983 when he was eighteen years old.

The next day when Elder met again with Rayson, the constable told Rayson that he had thought about their previous conversation and figured that the numbers and dates must be wrong. He said Rayson must have been seventeen years old in 1980, not fifteen, as he had calculated the day before. When they met again on December 10, Rayson said he remembered that he had passed through Vancouver before 1984; when he was seventeen he had hitchhiked from Edmonton to Los Angeles via Vancouver. Then, reflecting on his conversation with Detective Spall, Rayson asked Elder, "Did I tell you about the white van?" When Elder replied, "No," Rayson went on to say that he was talking to his girl-friend about the visit from the policeman and recalled that the policeman had said something about a white van, but he couldn't remember what.

I reviewed photographs of Jacobs' van taken shortly after it was towed from the Drake Hotel parking lot and lodged at the VPD vehicle compound in November 1980, and I noted that the van was actually grey with a white top, white interior, white bumpers, white mirrors and a white spare-tire cover with a red maple leaf on it. I spoke to Detective Spall on December 16 and confirmed that he had not made any comment regarding a van, white or otherwise, when he spoke to Rayson and the female party at the Arco Hotel. Their conversation had been specific, and the purpose had been only to set up a meeting where more details of the case would be discussed. However, knowledge of the involvement of a white van in these homicides was a critical piece of information that had come independently from Rayson. It supported my belief that he had specific knowledge of the crime, regardless of the fact that he said that he didn't remember what the officer had said about the van. On January 12, 2003, Rayson spoke to Constable Elder to discuss a possible relocation to Alberta to avoid further police enquiries. Rayson asked Elder, "What if I did do this when I was on bummers [narcotics]?" Elder told him he didn't care, but he needed to know what was going on so that the complication could be taken care of.

It was decided that Rayson would have to remain in British Columbia to deal with the problem.

With my Operational Plan in place, on January 17 I swore an affidavit and was granted an authorization to intercept all private communications between Rayson and Elder and/or Rayson and the "Crime Boss," in order to record conversations in which, we hoped, Rayson would reveal his knowledge of the murders of Eldon Jacobs and Marilyn Meersman. That same morning, prior to the recording of any conversations, Elder spoke to Rayson, who reflected that he was going to jail for a long time. He went on to say that when he was seventeen years old, he got picked up by a guy in the skids who offered him some money for sex. He went back to the guy's place and had some drinks. When the fellow left the house to pick up a bottle, Rayson started talking to a woman who also lived there. When the host returned with a bottle, they all had some drinks together. When the woman went upstairs to her room, Rayson got pissed off. He told the guy he was going to the bathroom but instead went to "the guy's room" and located a knife, and he demonstrated to Elder that the blade was about thirty centimetres long.

He was only going to rob Jacobs, but he ended up stabbing him in the back and the front. He went up to the girl's bedroom and told her the guy needed to see her. When she came downstairs, she saw the body, so he stabbed her in the back. When she fled up to her room again, he chased her and stabbed her again. He wiped down the area, hoping to obliterate his prints, then loaded up the van with stuff from the house. He drove the van to the Drake Hotel, noting that the building was no longer there. He wiped down the van prior to leaving it, tucking the knife into the seat. From his vantage point under the fire escape of the Drake Hotel, he had watched the police as they located the van.

Elder advised Rayson that he shouldn't worry about it and assured him that if there was something that needed to be taken care of, it would be taken care of. Between January 28 and 31 Elder travelled with Rayson to Kelowna to scout locations around Rock Creek and Osoyoos and probe the border, take GPS readings, make notations and take photos relating to suitable clandestine crossing points. On the morning of January 30 an impatient Rayson asked Elder if he had heard anything from the boss about a looming face-to-face meeting. He was advised that they should hear something in a couple of weeks. Captured on audio recording later that morning, a drunken, rambling Rayson admitted that he had killed the woman, adding, "That's another thing. Now my story's over. I got nothing more to say."

On February 6 we orchestrated a meeting between the "Crime Boss" and Rayson at an upscale hotel in Victoria, BC. As authorized by warrant, the room was wired for audio and video recording. In our adjoining room, popcorn and beverages were readied, anticipating a 2 p.m. performance, and a short time later Constable Elder escorted Rayson into the room to await the arrival of the Crime Boss. Over the next hour and twenty minutes, Rayson gave a clear and comprehensive description of how in 1980 he had murdered "Don," a gay man who picked him up downtown, and a female living upstairs, whose name he did not know. Rayson offered up information that could only have been known by the killer. This information included the following details:

"Don" was a man who picked Rayson up downtown and offered him money for sex. "We went for a ride, he took me back to his place and I knew what was going on, I knew he was queer, I knew what he wanted from me." Over the course of the investigation we discovered that it had not been generally known that Jacobs was homosexual.

The homicide took place in a rooming house. "This is a rooming house, like you know . . . a big house."

Don bought two bottles of "white liquor," possibly rum, which they drank. "It was . . . yeah, we sat in the house, we finished off a forty-pounder. And like I said, he went for another forty-pounder. It was white . . . white Bacardi, I guess." Investigators had found two empty vodka bottles on the kitchen floor.

The house had a Chinese motif. "He likes this Chinese stuff, he had a lot of Chinese ornaments." Investigators noted that "the room was furnished in an eastern motif. In keeping with this, the bird cage was made out of bamboo."

Rayson saw a chess set at the scene. One set of chessmen and a wooden case as well as two folding chess sets were located in Jacobs' stolen van.

Jacobs' bedroom was upstairs. There was one bathroom in the house and it was upstairs.

"I just positioned myself and I stabbed him twice in the back." During the initial attack, Jacobs had been stabbed in the back.

Rayson followed Meersman to her upstairs bedroom where he attacked and stabbed her to death. During the initial attack, Meersman had been stabbed in the back.

Rayson stole eight dollars from Jacobs. Jacobs' empty wallet was found at the scene.

He took nothing from Meersman. Her wallet was located on the floor and contained $14.83.

At the time of the attack, Meersman was wearing a housecoat and a nightgown, and he left Meersman's body exposed by lifting her clothing, then he covered her body with a blanket.

He wore gloves at the crime scene.

He ate food at the crime scene. "We had something to eat. And uh . . . I was . . . I was feeling pretty good, so we had something to eat." The investigators had reported that "on top of the stove was a tin containing one-sixth of a full portion of Italian-looking food."

Rayson said he had wiped down the crime scene. "I made sure I wiped it all, the glasses and everything."

Rayson said he had kicked in the doors of the other suites in an attempt to locate witnesses. "There was another person that lives in there but he was gone. He was out." The Crime Boss asked, "You weren't nervous about him coming back?" Rayson replied, "Obviously not, but I did kick his door in to check his room out."

Rayson said that one of the other tenants in the house was out of town. "It was a big house, like a boarding house. He's got one room and uh . . . there was a person in the other room but uh . . . he was . . . he was out of town and then there was her in the other room."

Rayson said that Jacobs owned the murder weapon. It was a "Chinese dagger, there was no groove, a straight blade, sharp on both sides." Rayson said he left the murder weapon tucked behind the backrest and driver's seat of Jacobs' van.

Rayson said Jacobs was six foot three: "He's a tall fellow, about six-three, grey hair." Jacobs was six foot five and a half.

The "Crime Boss" asked, "Who would he look like out of the movie stars you know? Offhand?" Rayson answered, "I don't know, Donald Sutherland maybe." I thought there was a similarity and included a photo of Donald Sutherland in the evidence package, allowing the judge to make the comparison himself.

Given that there was no murder weapon located in the evidence repository, I found a resident expert on knives at a local historical military collectors show held in Burnaby. This man, a doctor, had written two books on fighting knives; he provided expert testimony regarding the Fairbairn-Sykes commando dagger and brought a duplicate to the court-room. His testimony indicated that the origins of the knife were based on the Shanghai fighting knife, which saw service with British commando units, post 1940. "This is a slightly post-war commando dagger. In the late 1940s Sykes and Fairbairn were in the Shanghai Police in what would be called the SWAT unit of today."

The video-recorded confession offered a compelling description of how Rayson murdered Eldon Jacobs and Marilyn Meersman. The justification for the murders was split between robbery and Rayson losing control of his anger because he thought Meersman reminded him of his old girlfriend. After the interview with the Crime Boss, Rayson travelled back to the Lower Mainland and took a room at the Comfort Inn on No. 3 Road in Richmond. On February 7 I met with members of the VPD Emergency Response Team (ERT) in Richmond to coordinate the arrest. Constable Elder phoned Rayson and asked him to come out in front of the motel, where he would meet him. When Rayson appeared in the breezeway area, he was taken into custody by members of the ERT. Having observed the arrest, I attended the scene and formally arrested, chartered and warned Rayson for the murders of Eldon Jacobs and Marilyn Meersman. I hand-cuffed him with the same cuffs I had used in the arrest of

The Emergency Response Team was deployed to make initial contact with a "Centrefold Murders" suspect outside a motel in Richmond, BC. I made the formal arrest, detailed the particulars of the charge and took custody using these handcuffs.

Jim Strachan for the murder of Ethan Hughes, then I phoned Marilyn's mother and told her that her daughter's killer had finally been captured.

Rayson initially pled not guilty, but changed his mind when confronted with the weight of evidence he had essentially given against himself. He received two life sentences with no chance of parole for fifteen years and did not receive any credit for time spent in custody awaiting trial. The motive of theft and the elimination of witnesses was straightforward, but there never was any explanation for why Rayson arranged Marilyn Meersman's body in such a macabre tableau.

Murder at the Ho Ho in Chinatown

On March 17, 1989, King Yok Lum, an eighty-two-year-old woman, was found dead in her room above the Ho Ho Restaurant at 102 East Pender Street in Vancouver. Mrs. Lum appeared to have died of natural causes. She was slumped over in her chair with her scarf wrapped around her neck. There was no indication that anybody else had been in the room at the time of her death, and the room was secure. However, investigators were later called to the morgue, as an autopsy had determined that the victim died of a ligature strangulation that fractured her hyoid bone. Follow-up investigation revealed that the victim's purse and ring were missing. The last person to see the victim alive was Charles Gavin, a Native man who lived upstairs, and he could offer no insight into the cause of death.

Three years later, in June 1992, I investigated the robbery of Frank Hardy, a pastor at 6025 St. George Street in East Vancouver. Hardy was a small, eighty-year-old man who was attacked from behind by his assailant and pushed down the stairs of his church. He had then suffered seventeen blows to the head that exposed his brain and left him in a coma. The surgeon offered such a dire prognosis that I was prompted to take a "dying declaration," but when Hardy came out of his coma, he had no recollection of the incident. Some days later the nursing staff notified us that he was lucid and now had a clear recollection of events. I interviewed the staff prior to conducting an interview with the victim and was advised that he would probably not recover from his injuries. I approached the reverend and discussed the fact that he would probably not survive his injuries, a procedure that is requisite in taking a "dying declaration" that is an exception to the hearsay rule of evidence. Though insensitive, it allows a verbal statement made by a dying victim to stand with the force of law in court where death precludes making the statement in person. The reverend considered what I had said and commented, "The doctor says I am getting better."

Hardy then went on to describe a Native male who had been hanging around the church, pestering him for money. One morning after he had again turned this party away, the man pushed him down the stairs and pounded on his head with a club, robbing him and leaving him for dead. Our follow-up investigation identified Charles Gavin as the assailant.

That September, three months after the attack on Frank Hardy, Gavin was arrested in the Okanagan and transported back to Vancouver. In the course of conducting his interview, I noted the presence of a small amount of blood on his shirt. I seized the clothing and had it processed for analysis, but forensic testing determined that the blood didn't relate to the robbery of Hardy, so the clothing was destroyed. At the time we did not connect that Gavin had been near the scene of the murder at the Ho Ho three years earlier.

At the end of the interview, he was advised regarding the charges and uttered, almost silently, "Oh well, if you play, you got to pay." That comment, when related to the courts, was instrumental in winning a conviction.

Meanwhile, on August 13, 1992, Ray Alcock, a seventy-eight-year-old retired mechanical engineer, had been found dead in a pool of blood on the floor of his apartment at a rooming house at 1346 Cotton Drive. Alcock had been beaten around the head, suffering nineteen identifiable strikes by a undetermined weapon that was rectangular in shape, about six centimetres at the base and tapering to about five centimetres at the front. There were two smudged fingerprints on the lower wall area just above the body, but there was insufficient detail to process the fingerprints through the national database.

While some other members of the Homicide Unit had also attended the June 15 robbery of Reverend Hardy, pending the demise of the victim, my partner and I were handed the initial investigation of the case. No link was made between it and the Alcock case, although they took place less than two months apart. In 1997 an undercover operation was mounted on another possible suspect, but he denied any involvement and passed a polygraph to prove his innocence. However, that same year, the fingerprints found on the wall above Ray Alcock's body were re-processed, and they identified Charles Gavin as a person of interest.

In 2003 the Historical Homicide Unit started a lifestyle investigation into the background of Gavin, who was now living in an apartment on the eastern edge of Vancouver's Chinatown. On May 27 an RCMP undercover officer made initial contact with Gavin, asking him to assist him in finding a female in a photograph. Gavin failed to make a second contact with the officer as had been agreed, explaining that he had been up in the Yukon and had been unavailable for work. At the conclusion of the lengthy undercover operation, Gavin disclosed to Mr. Big that he had committed three murders in Vancouver, but he said, "I never left no shit, no pile of dirt where I would leave a trail." He went on to say that one of his murders took place in the area of Grant and Commercial. "It was a big rooming house. I had to go and do it fast, and— boom!—be out of there." In the course of the undercover operation, Gavin took the undercover operator on a tour of the Cotton Drive crime scene, disclosing that he had kicked Alcock to death with the heel of his cowboy boot. He said he killed him because "he's the type of guy who would say, if I left him alive, 'I let a guy rob me, and he's got my money and I marked it.'" I purchased a pair of cowboy boots in Gavin's size, and forensic testing in blocks of clay showed that they would have left a wound pattern similar to that on Alcock's head.

By this time, Gavin was so taken in by his new crime family that he asked his undercover handler to stand for him as best man at his upcoming wedding, and wrote him a poem called "Young Brother." He now claimed that while in the Yukon he had taken one or more people out into the woods and killed them, but had made these incidents look like hunting accidents. On September 6 he told the undercover operator that he had killed an Indian male at the Ho Ho, leaving the body in a position that would cause the police to believe that the victim had died as a result of an overdose. However, in the history of Vancouver there has only been one murder at the Ho Ho, that of King Yok Lum. On another occasion Gavin told his undercover handler that he had killed five men and three women, on another that he had collected five scalps. Many of his stories were so outrageous they defied logic.

On January 19, 2004, we arrested Charles Gavin at the train station at Main Street and Terminal Avenue. As I read the charges, astonished tourists stood back, and I heard one of them say, "Hey, it's one of those cold case arrests." Gavin phoned his "young brother" from jail to request assistance.

The position of defence at trial was that Gavin was a pathological liar who told "whoppers, big lies, that he is grandiose and flamboyant and cannot be believed." In her summary, the judge said:

There is no question that I am left with a reasonable doubt as to the guilt of the accused on this charge. There are many troubling aspects to this case which leave me with that doubt. There are also many troubling aspects of this case that leave me with suspicion. The one aspect that does not leave me with any doubt is the nature of the undercover operation by the police. The police effort was extensive and commendable, but they appear to have been dealing with a loose cannon.

She concluded, "The Crown has failed to prove this charge beyond a reasonable doubt. Accordingly, I must find the accused not guilty of this charge."

The Case of Pamela Darlington and Gale Weys
I was seventeen in the summer of 1973 when I met nineteen-year-old Pamela Darlington. She was a very pretty girl about five feet four inches tall, weighing 125 pounds, and she had straight reddish-brown hair. She had travelled from her hometown of Kamloops to visit her aunt, uncle and cousin (who was a good friend of mine) in East Vancouver for the holidays. At the time I lived on East 20th Avenue and they lived down the lane closer to Trout Lake on East 19th. As a seventeen-year-old lifeguard, driving a blue 1968 Volkswagen Beetle (way before those cars were trendy), I don't think I made much of an impression on her.

But Pamela Darlington disappeared in Kamloops on November 6 of that same year. Around 9:30 p.m., she had stopped off at her apartment on Knox Street in the neighbourhood of Tranquille on the north side of the Thompson River and told her roommate that she was going to hitchhike over to a pub in Kamloops to meet with friends, because she was leaving the next day for a new job in Whistler. She never arrived there.

Gail Weys was another nineteen-year-old white female about two inches taller than Pamela, and weighing about five pounds less, but she also had straight reddish-blond hair. Just after 10 p.m. on the evening of October 19, 1973, Gail had finished her shift at the Wells Grey Hotel in Clearwater and set out to hitchhike to Kamloops, 125 kilometres south, for a scheduled visit with her family. When she never arrived, her parents were understandably concerned and contacted police.

As a result, investigators assumed that the body found on the banks of the South Thompson on November 7 was that of Gail Weys. The body was found face down in the water, just downstream from the Red Bridge. Her face had been disfigured by her attacker, who had left the scene with her clothing and identification. The police called Gail Weys' father to the morgue, where he made a positive identification. But after he left the room, he hesitated and said, "Wait a moment." Then he explained to the investigators that Gail had been coming to Kamloops to have some dental work done on a chipped tooth. He wanted to look at the body again just to make completely sure. To the astonishment of the detectives, the father checked the teeth to find them intact. This girl was not his daughter, but her virtual twin, Pamela Darlington, who had disappeared on November 6. Gail Weys' body was found after the snow melted, on April 6, 1974, just off the old highway near the small community of Blackpool, about seven kilometres south of Clearwater.

Soon after the murders occurred, one person emerged as a primary suspect. Jim Damien was an aluminum gutter salesman, who at the time of the murders had an office virtually across the street from Darlington's apartment on Knox Street near Tranquille Road. He was a convincted rapist and lifelong criminal whose job required that he travel the Thompson Okanagan area selling his product. Knowing he was inclined to pick up hitchhikers, investigators checked his sales records and were able to establish that he was near Clearwater at the time of Weys' murder and in Kamloops at the time of Darlington's.

Calls were received on the tip line and detectives were told of a scrapbook of photos and news clippings relating to the missing hitchhikers that had been kept by Damien, but this material was never located. One informant said that on the morning after Darlington's murder, Damien had been seen with cuts on his arms. Another said that after the murders Damien fled to Vancouver Island, where he set fire to his car in an effort to destroy evidence. At about the time Damien arrived on Vancouver Island, a young woman named Carmen Robinson had gone missing from West Burnside Road in View Royal just north of Victoria. The bus driver had dropped Robinson off about a quarter mile from her home, and he saw her walk toward her house from the bus stop. He was the last person to see her alive. Her body was never found; she remains listed as a missing person.

Periodically, Pamela Darlington's family asked me if there had been any breaks in the case. Her Aunt Isabel wrote to me: "We didn't see much of Pam since her childhood. She was a very outgoing and friendly girl, never shy or afraid of strangers." When I was assigned to the Unsolved Homicide Unit, I thought I would have a closer look at the file.

One would think that in a case of murder as brutal as this one there would be very few likely suspects. In fact, we had a long list, though Damien had remained at the top of it for more than thirty years. On January 9, 2003, I gave our staff sergeant a summary of the two unsolved homicides and received his authorization to move forward with an investigation. I attended the Kamloops detachment and took possession of the original evidence, which had all been properly catalogued and was essentially in original condition. All of the physical evidence was then reprocessed for DNA comparisons, but the results were ultimately of no use to us. Contained in the file was a picture of one of the detectives holding up a large rock that had been used as a weapon in the Darlington murder. He was not wearing gloves, as the irregular surface of the rock would not lend itself to fingerprint analysis, but in modern times that rock would have been valuable, as it would be an excellent carrier of the killer's DNA since the rough surface would have held abraded skin cells.

Although I was involved in several other operations, my partner and I spent about a year doing a background investigation into this case and concluded that there was a high probability that Damien was the culprit. On June 7, 2004, I decided to formally move ahead with a request for an undercover operation. I would write up an operational plan, craft a Part VI (wiretap) warrant, be responsible for the Crown Counsel Report and deal with the exhibits and the media. My partner would deal with disclosure (thank God), thirty-day reports, the budget, file management and timelines.

On October 25 I travelled to Winnipeg, where I spoke to the corporal (now long retired) who had been in charge of the Darlington investigation. He said that, while the body was found in the morning, it appeared that it had been dropped into the water the previous evening and that it would not have been unnatural for it to have gone unseen until the afternoon. Though the body was close to the boat ramp, there was a skiff of ice on the river, so nobody would have been using a boat that day. His recollection was that there was no current in that specific area, but that if the body had been pushed a few more feet toward the centre of the river, it would have caught the current and travelled downstream.

The Kamloops RCMP had not investigated the Weys murder, as it had occurred outside of the municipal boundary in a different RCMP jurisdiction. But the retired corporal drew my attention to a photo of Colleen MacMillen that he had in his notebook and told me that she had been murdered on August 9, 1974, just south of 100 Mile House. He said that if Darlington and Weys looked like twins, MacMillen could have been their younger sister, a shorter version of the other two victims. MacMillen was a strawberry blond with long straight hair. He went on to say that between October 1969 and August 1974, there were seven similar homicides involving young girls in the Thompson Okanagan area. These were Gloria Moody, Gail Weys, Pamela Darlington, an unidentified female from Valemount, an unidentified female from Naramata, Christine Lequesne and Colleen MacMillen.

By October 2004 we were in the middle of a lifestyle investigation into the background and behaviour of Damien, who was then living in North Vancouver. His morning routine was to drive to the A&W on Mountain Highway, read the paper and then drive around completing various chores for the rest of the day. On October 29 I followed him into the A&W and sat a few seats away to overhear an argument he was having with his female companion. Due to a lack of manpower, I had the RCMP's Special O Surveillance Team with us that day, and one of their operators was working with me. When Damien got up with the woman and left, I screened the operator as he seized the cup Damien had been drinking from. I took custody of it and later processed it for DNA analysis. On another occasion, one of the other units had just finished a Mr. Big undercover operation that was prominently displayed on the front page of the *Province* newspaper. That day I beat Damien to the restaurant and seized all of the papers that were in the rack, replacing them with copies of *The Globe and Mail* and the *Vancouver Sun* that I had acquired.

At that time I had heard that Special O's credibility had been severely compromised by sloppy technique, which was causing surveillance to get frequently burned. In fact, it had become common knowledge that if you wanted to dump a slow file, you would call in Special O to do some surveillance, they would take a burn and you could jettison the case. But I didn't have any specific knowledge of this problem and had worked closely with them years earlier, so I was willing to take the risk. However, one day I worked with a Special O supervisor who had just acquired a large camera that he thought was suitable for surveillance. We followed a female party from a secondary residence to a strip mall on Mountain Highway where she went into a bank. The Mountie pulled into a parking spot close to the bank and positioned the car so that we would be able to see her when she left. As she exited the bank, he held the camera up over the steering wheel, clearly visible to her and anybody else in the parking lot, and then took her picture. She stopped, screamed and ran to her car. Squealing her tires, she sped around the parking lot and stopped behind us, where, in the side mirror, I saw her writing down our licence plate number. I turned to my driver, "I guess we're pretty much finished for the day?"

However, after a very difficult, complex and comprehensive lifestyle investigation, a member of the undercover team made initial contact with Damien on February 16, 2005, more than two years after I first considered taking on the case. And Damien was soon being run all across western Canada, completing task after task as he worked his way up through Mr. Big's organization. He proved to be a thoroughly despicable individual who, when asked on March 4 by his undercover handler why he had been drinking and was in such good spirits, answered that he was celebrating the deaths of the four RCMP officers who had been killed in Mayerthorpe, Alberta, the previous day. I don't know how you could hear such poisonous bile and not lash out, but it stands as testament to the professionalism of the undercover officer that he carried on without reacting.

One of the final scenarios involved our crime family kidnapping a female (an undercover RCMP member) who had betrayed the organization. Damien was involved in her initial capture in Winnipeg, then she was transported to the basement of an abandoned farmhouse in Lavenham, 144 kilometres away. The farmhouse was actually owned by the parents of one of the undercover officers and was sitting derelict since they had built a new home on a nearby property. The whole of the old house was in disrepair, mildewed wallpaper hanging from the walls, linoleum peeling up from the plywood floors, plumbing fixtures scavenged by thieves. The basement looked like something out of a Stephen King movie, everything completely covered in cobwebs, broken tools scattered across a bench, an antique prosthetic leg leaning against the wall. And when Damien and the team arrived, the kidnapped female, who appeared like she had been severely beaten, was chained to the central supporting post of the basement. (I take credit for her Coca Cola hair rinse that left the impression of unkempt sleaze.)

Damien's handler escorted him to the basement along with a third crime-family member. The handler indicated that he hadn't really decided what he was going to do with the traitor, and it was understood that Damien's role would be just to stand by in case any assistance was needed. (I was positioned about half a mile away, monitoring the scenario while trying out the new Steiner binoculars on which I had just spent all of my overtime cash—$1,100—at the Cabela's store in Winnipeg, attempting to see if I could locate any of those big Manitoba white-tail deer I had heard so much about.) Questions and answers between the handler and the female ended with Damien being told to go back upstairs. As he passed the kidnapped Mountie, he grabbed her by the hair and told her to "smarten up," then he continued up the stairs. A few minutes passed after the handler joined Damien in the kitchen, then the two heard a single shot of a .357-calibre pistol resonate throughout the building, indicating that the problem in the basement had been resolved.

The undercover contingent headed back to Winnipeg. My partner, the support team and I relocated to the farmhouse, where we had a few beers to celebrate an extremely successful operation, the immediate prelude to the Mr. Big scenario. However, a concern expressed by the RCMP sergeant was that the target had actually touched the female undercover operator, signalling our failure to control the physical environment, a failure that could have endangered the operator, who was bound by chains, unable to protect herself. The issue was discussed at length, and we concluded that, given the tightness of the crowded basement, it was just something that could not be avoided without compromising the reality of the scenario. In any case, the female undercover operator said that she had no concerns. A concern that I did not vocalize at the time was that when Damien grabbed the operator by the hair and told her to smarten up, he appeared to be showing concern for her welfare. This was completely inconsistent with his psychological profile—that of a homicidal sociopath. I decided that I was reading too much into a brief comment. In any case, he didn't display any remorse about participating in her abduction and what he thought was her subsequent execution.

On July 6, 2005, the investigative team descended on Victoria B.C., where we set up adjacent rooms in my favourite hotel to do the Mr. Big scenario. Damien arrived to plead, cajole and beg Mr. Big for a position in the criminal empire, but he stated clearly and unequivocally that he had nothing to do with the murder of any girls in the province. After the scenario, I met with Mr. Big (an outstanding operator and the same officer who had listened to the Ethan Hughes murder confession) and he told me, "Wayne, he's saying he didn't do those murders." We discussed the matter and decided that we would take the extraordinary step of having Damien take a polygraph to prove he didn't commit the murders.

Damien was told that the days of extracting confessions with a baseball bat or waterboarding had been replaced by more civilized methods of establishing the truth. Instead, Mr. Big had an ex-KGB officer working for the organization who conducted lie-detector examinations on behalf of his criminal empire. Evgeni Volokov conducted his polygraph and established on the balance of probability that Damien was telling the truth. I was astounded. The purpose of running an operation was either to identify and charge those guilty of serious crimes or to clear the innocent from suspicion. I always prefer the former outcome over the latter. For the past thirty years Damien had been the hands-down favourite as the prime suspect in three murders. Now we knew that the murderer was still out there.

The Follow-up: Fast-forward to 2012

The Provincial Unsolved Homicide Unit—which had previously processed DNA in this case with negative results—re-submitted DNA from the Colleen MacMillen homicide to an international police database. Due to advances in technology, on May 3, 2012, a forensic lab in Oregon was able to confirm a DNA match to Bobby Fowler (in this case, I have given the murderer's real name), a sex offender who had been employed in the Prince George area in 1974. News reports speculate that he was a strong suspect in the murders of Pamela Darlington and Gail Weys. Fowler had no criminal record in Canada, and except for the fact he was known to have worked in the area, there is no indication that he ever had any contact with the police here in British Columbia. In 2006 Fowler died in prison, where he was serving time for a serious assault.

Cal Marriott

On October 27, 1998, Cal Marriot was found beaten to death in his home in Spallumcheen, an agricultural community lying between Vernon and Enderby located in British Columbia's idyllic Spallumcheen Valley. Police investigators concluded that the murder related to an argument over drugs, as 387 marijuana plants were found on the property. Theodore Grant, one of Marriott's associates, was immediately suspected of the crime, but police lacked evidence to support a charge.

The Provincial Unsolved Homicide Unit had our first meeting regarding the file on October 17, 2005, and it was decided that my unit would be responsible for the lifestyle investigation and providing manpower in support of the undercover operation. The last address for Grant was at a residence in Port Coquitlam, but he had vacated that house and been seen in the area pushing a two-wheeled shopping cart full of his possessions. It is extremely difficult to follow a transient ragpicker as he meanders through various suburban neighbourhoods because the officers conducting the surveillance don't have the ambient foot and vehicular traffic that can be used as an effective shield.

It wasn't until December 7 that contact between the undercover member and the target was finally made and a relationship established. But the target failed to follow up with a meeting as he had committed to do, so on January 12, 2006, we orchestrated another bump, and by mid-January the undercover program was in full swing, and Grant was involved in transporting property to Nanaimo. Over the course of the next three months, the target disclosed that the reason that he had moved to the Vancouver area and off of the grid was because the RCMP had been harassing him about a murder. He thought that this would be the best way to derail the investigation. In fact, what he thought was true, but he should have moved east a province or two where it would have been much more difficult to track him down. On March 29 Grant confessed to Mr. Big, and at the Law Courts in Vernon, BC, he was sentenced to nine years in prison.

This case was essentially the most standard investigation that the Unsolved Homicide Unit conducted. Since its inception, the unit's mandate has been to use all legal means available to bring killers to justice. The best and most effective way of securing such convictions turned out to be the deployment of undercover officers, and I used them in every investigation I was involved in.

Flares That Go off in the Night

In the course of investigating hundreds of major (and many more minor) crimes, I have noticed several common themes that tend to indicate guilt. These have greater significance than red flags. They are more like flares going off in the night.

When the detective interviewing a homicide suspect makes a superfluous and inappropriate notation in the case file that the subject is simply not capable of committing a murder, that suspect is probably guilty. I have seen it happen on two occasions and both times the suspect turned out to be a serial killer. Second, when the term "alibi" never

Provincial Unsolved Homicide Unit shoulder patches.

previously surfaced in conversation with the suspect, and he uses that word to describe where he was at the time of the crime, he is probably guilty. Third, when asked whether or not he committed the crime, instead of denying involvement, the suspect says, "Why would I do that?" he is probably guilty. Innocent people lash out uncompromisingly at false accusations.

In the case of a very serious crime, I learned to ask the suspect what he thought should happen to the perpetrator. If he minimizes the penalty by suggesting minor incarceration, therapy or counselling rather than lethal injection or the electric chair, he was probably guilty. And when a suspect was cooperative, admitted being a witness but denied involvement in a crime, I had him write up a statement describing what he knew. I would be vague about the specific type of information that should be included as well as where the narrative should begin and end. In the case of an innocent witness, the crime would be described in the first third of the statement and that would be the focus of the rest of the story. In the perpetrator's rendition, the first two-thirds of the statement would relate to all manner of irrelevant details. In the last third there would be a cursory reference to the incident, which would minimize his personal involvement. (There is actually a field of study related to this phenomenon; it is called statement analysis.)

The RCMP do a lot of things right. They have outstanding undercover teams, emergency response teams and dog squad teams, all of whom I have worked with many times. I don't know how effective their homicide teams are, as I have only worked with the Historical Homicide units, who are outstanding. What the RCMP is incapable of doing is municipal policing. The other units work so effectively because by their nature they respond well to a military structure, which is what the RCMP is—a regiment in the Canadian military. Officers are not given badge numbers; they are issued regimental numbers. Senior officers pledge fealty to their management team in Ottawa, not to municipal police boards. The problem with this structure when it comes to municipal policing—and to a certain extent in all of the other policing that they do—is that every officer is just passing through. There is no bond or commitment to the community. In fact, members are discouraged from policing the communities in which they were raised, and while I worked with the RCMP, there was a mandatory transfer policy in place: after serving a fixed number of years in one community, officers were required to transfer to another. Promotion, because the officer was applying for a posted position rather than a simple promotion, normally resulted in a transfer to another area.

The observation I made while working at the RCMP satellite office in Surrey was that police officers blew through the place like leaves blowing through the forest. In my five and a half years there, I had three different RCMP bosses. One thing that did stand out in my mind regarding major-crime investigations involving the RCMP is that they have no collective investigative memory relating to the work. When dealing with a cold case, the officer who did the initial major-crime investigation is long gone, as are any of the people who conducted follow-ups.

In the Vancouver Police Department, if you asked, "Remember that case eight or ten years ago when the suspect tried to strangle that woman with a telephone cord?" several people might remember the file even if they weren't directly involved in it. They might remember it just because it was unique and perhaps even be able to identify the original investigator. With the RCMP there would be no way that anyone in that office would have even been in the province eight or ten years ago. They could have been in Regina on the Musical Ride or checking crab traps in Anchor Point, Newfoundland, but the rotational mandate pretty much means that they wouldn't have been anywhere near this detective office.

This is not a problem that can easily be fixed. Even if the policy was changed and officers were allowed to stay in a community of their choosing, there would be subsequent damage to their careers, and perhaps there should be. The Force is federal by definition, so it stands to reason that experiencing the largest number of varied opportunities offered by multiple postings throughout the country would enhance promotional potential. There is nothing inherently wrong with packing up and leaving every three or four years, but the model does not benefit a community that is policed by transient officers. A federal-policing model does not synchronize with the municipal one. It would be like having the FBI offer a discounted policing model to some American states and cities, but it is a non-starter that we in British Columbia have somehow embraced. I think that the differences in the two forces can be most simply distinguished by examination of their mottos. The VPD motto, as seen on its official crest, is *Servamus* or Service. The RCMP motto is *Maintiens le Droit* or Maintain the Right, which I interpret to mean maintain the status quo or support the established authority. The two mandates have absolutely nothing in common.

The Transit Police, 2006–09

On March 10, 2006, I had completed thirty-one years of service with the Vancouver Police Department. As I had joined the force at nineteen years of age, I was qualified to leave with a full pension, which amounted to just over 75 percent of my base wage at age fifty. (I want to thank the Vancouver Police Union for negotiating such a solid return on all of the contributions I made throughout my career.) I felt that the work I was doing at the Provincial Unsolved Homicide Unit was so interesting that I was prepared to stay longer, but that spring I got a phone call from Dan Dureau of Cushman Racing fame, who was now a commissioned officer with the Transit Police. He advised me that the training officer's job had come open. The position had been posted with no success internally and now was going public. When I told him that I was happy where I was, he told me to get a pencil and sit down so we could talk about the benefits of pulling a full pension with the Vancouver Police Department while adding to it a training officer's wage from the Transit Police.

I advised the VPD I would be retiring on July 31, and at the end of June I put a thirty-day countdown calendar outside my office. The final page of the calendar read: "Elvis has left the building."

As it turned out, Elvis returned to the building after taking the summer off, and in September 2006 I was hired as the Vancouver Transit Police training officer. It had taken me seventeen years to get promoted first to corporal and then to sergeant with the VPD. In just seventeen weeks I had my sergeant's interview with Transit. The constables from the Training Section huddled around the closed conference room door as I kept the personnel officer in stitches with a stand-up comedy routine that went on for less than twenty minutes. I enthralled her with my "idiot factor" theory, piqued her interest with an overview of how the RCMP undercover unit had become so valuable solving old murders, and when I ran out the generally accepted practice regarding problem solving, she asked, "What course did you learn that on?" My response was, "All of them." At this point the whole board was keeling over with laughter. At the end of the interview I was told to leave the room and they would be with me shortly. My compatriots said, "That interview was less than twenty minutes long, which is either really good or really bad." A few minutes later the chair of the meeting came out to congratulate me: I was the new sergeant in charge of Internal Affairs (Professional Standards).

I had a plaque with this Latin phrase on it nailed unobtrusively to the wall of my office: *Quoniam non eram ibi. I non fecit. Im non hic nunc.* Nobody ever asked what it meant.

The translation is: I wasn't there. I didn't do it. I'm not here now.

One of my jobs was to lecture new recruits regarding the British Columbia Police Act. I'm guessing Transit management hadn't heard about Vancouver's restraining order forbidding me to talk to young, impressionable police officers. Here is an excerpt from one of my lectures:

> One thing that always comes up is gratuities. What happens when a restaurant owner refuses to allow police officers to pay for coffee or a small meal? The standard response is: leave a tip for the waitress equal to the cost of the meal. For other kinds of gratuities, consult with your policy and procedure manual and find out what it has to say.
>
> For Transit Police there is a zero tolerance policy when it comes to gratuities. For Vancouver PD, the policy was as follows: if you received a gratuity in the course of your duties, you were to write up a memo detailing the circumstances surrounding the incident and forward the report and the gratuity to the superintendent, who would decide on a course of action.

I'd tell my students about a successful resolution to a violent kidnapping while I was serving in the Major Crime Unit. The victim's father, a wealthy Hong Kong businessman, requested that my partner and I come to his home, where he would offer us gifts of appreciation. After ringing the door of his Shaughnessy mansion, we were shown into the sitting room and awaited the arrival of the grateful patriarch. I had decided that I wanted my new Jaguar convertible to be British racing green and was about to let him know my preference when he presented me with a pen set and a business card holder. The desk set had an ornate rectangular base made of jade

This sterling silver cardholder was a gift from a wealthy Hong Kong businessman in appreciation for successfully resolving the kidnapping of his young son. I later used it as lecture material while serving as sergeant in charge of Internal Affairs for the Vancouver Transit Police.

with a rampant dragon and Chinese characters engraved on the surface. Two silver receptacles held matching Sheaffer pens with a brushed gunmetal finish accented by palladium and gold-plate trim. One was a fountain pen with an inter-changeable flexible medium nib, suitable for calligraphy, and the other was a standard roller ball. The cardholder was made of sterling silver and had the Hong Kong Police Department medallion affixed to the surface. I returned to my office, wrote up the requisite report and forwarded it and the two gifts to my superintendent.

A week later I got the cardholder back through the departmental mail. I never saw the jade desk set again, but when I occasionally visit the Vancouver Police Department's executive floors, I make it a practice to glance nonchalantly into the offices of the Senior Management Team, hoping to catch a glimpse of those pens.